"Those of us who work in the child welfare system quickly become experts in human suffering. We live and work in a world that is foreign to most. But in order for our society to accept responsibility for helping and healing these children, their courageous stories must be told. Holly Schlaack has so eloquently shared the heartbreak, misery, and sometimes joy that is the daily life of those who live and work in the system. She has used her case-by-case experience and her passion for these children to attempt to influence public policy by capturing our hearts. This book brings the reader into the real world of child welfare, a world we all need to learn more about if we are to save these wonderful children."

—*Cindy S. Lederman, Presiding Judge of the Miami-Dade Juvenile Court*

"Foster parents, like birth parents, can be both good and bad, no matter what their own background or place in society. Holly Schlaack does a fantastic job in revealing foster parents who look at foster children and see dollar signs, while many others are dedicated people who see foster children as missing something only they can provide: love. Her book gives concrete steps we can all take to insure there are no more kids like Marcus Fiesel who is remembered more for the horrible way in which he died rather than an uplifting story about how he lived. I highly recommend her book."

—*Mark E. Piepmeier, Prosecuting Attorney in the murder trial against the foster parents of Marcus Fiesel*

"The best thing about this book is the hope it presents. While it's the real story on the foster care program in America—no punches pulled—it's also a roadmap to making things better. It's engaging, it tugs at the heartstrings, and it's a hopeful look at how every child can have an actual childhood. If you care about children at all, you must read what Holly Schlaack has written."

—*Laren Bright, Award-Winning Writer of Children's Animation*

THE REAL STORY ON FOSTER CARE AND REAL SOLUTIONS FOR MAKING IT BETTER

WHEN MARCUS FIESEL'S STORY of torture, abandonment, and a slow, agonizing death came to light, it was not exactly news to Holly Schlaack. She was an insider in the foster care system and Marcus' horrible experience was just an extreme example of how she knew the system could fail.

Happily, Holly had also seen some success stories that were as inspiring as Marcus' story was appalling. So she set out to create a way for there to be more happy endings. This book is part of the effort.

Invisible Kids tells the stories of many children and foster families. It tells them straight and backs them up with statistics and facts that show why the system works, why it doesn't, and where it needs help. It describes the special program Holly herself created for the early identification of red flags in the lives of infants and toddlers. It details how this program, ProKids Building Blocks, is making a difference, with specialized training and home visitation checklists that assist in objectifying warning signs that might otherwise go unnoticed. It also identifies more than a dozen ways, large and small, anyone can apply to make a difference.

When stories reach the news, an enraged public often jumps to conclusions or springs to solutions that are superficial and do not take into account the real issues. *Invisible Kids* goes in depth so practical approaches and real solutions can surface.

It is too easy to think that all children have a reasonably happy childhood. Sadly, we learn, some children have no childhood at all. In this day and age this is neither necessary nor acceptable. If you care about children, here are ideas to put your caring into action.

ABOUT THE AUTHOR

Holly Schlaack stands strong and tall as a voice for children who often have none. Deeply moved by the plight of invisible children in the foster care system, she has tirelessly advocated in the courts on their behalf. She has put her time and energy on the line, acting as a Guardian Ad Litem (GAL), and gone the extra mile to ensure the best interests of abused and neglected children are served. Holly also has extensive experience supervising Court Appointed Special Advocates (CASAs), mentoring and encouraging them to excellence in assisting the children in their charge.

In 2000, Holly developed Building Blocks: Specialized Advocacy for Abused and Neglected Infants and Toddlers. This innovative program has become a model of quality advocacy for CASA Programs around the country and was awarded special recognition by the Ohio Attorney General's Office. Holly co-founded and served as President of the Southwest Chapter of the Ohio Association for Infant Mental Health (OAIMH), served on the state board of OAIMH, and has presented at various conferences regarding young children and the juvenile court system. Holly and her husband, Ed, live in Cincinnati, Ohio. They are the devoted parents of three children, Hanna, Grace, and Ben.

INVISIBLE KIDS

INVISIBLE KIDS

Marcus Fiesel's Legacy

One short life, one terrible death and 12 things
YOU can do to improve the lives of foster children

HOLLY SCHLAACK

**ADVOCACY
PUBLISHING**
Cincinnati, Ohio

This publication is designed to educate and provide general information regarding the subject matter covered. It is not intended to replace the counsel of other professional advisors. The reader is encouraged to consult with his or her own advisors regarding specific situations. While the author has taken reasonable precautions in the preparation of this book and believes the facts presented within the book are accurate, neither the publisher nor author assumes any responsibility for errors or omissions. The author and publisher specifically disclaim any liability resulting from the use or application of the information contained in this book. The information within this book is not intended to serve as emotional or therapeutic advice related to individual situations.

Editor's Note: With the exception of Marcus Fiesel and the people related to his story who became public figures by virtue of their involvement in this newsworthy story, the names and other identifying information of other people portrayed in this book have been changed to protect their identities. Any resemblance to persons living or dead is purely coincidental.

Advocacy Publishing
7672 Montgomery Rd. #221
Cincinnati, Ohio 45236

Second Edition
Publisher's Cataloging-In-Publication

Schlaack, Holly.
    Invisible kids : Marcus Fiesel's legacy : one short life, one terrible
    death and 12 things you can do to improve the lives of foster
    children / Holly Schlaack. -- 2nd ed. -- Cincinnati, Ohio : Advocacy
    Publishing, c2010.
        p. ; cm.
        ISBN: 978-0-615-22976-8
        Includes bibliographical references.

        1. Foster children--United States. 2. Foster home care--United
        States. 3. Child welfare--United States. 4. Foster children--Abuse
        of--United States--Prevention. 5. Foster children--Services for--
        United States. I. Title.

HV875.55 .S35 2009   2008939744
362.73/30973--dc22   0801

Printed in the United States of America on acid-free paper.

Cover and book design: Patricia Bacall
Author Photo: Christine Neitzke
Book Consultant: Ellen Reid

For Marcus

May the power of your story ignite hearts to change and hands to help the thousands of children who suffer.

CONTENTS

ACKNOWLEDGMENTS

One of the overriding themes of this book is the importance of relationships. This is an overriding theme in my life as well. I value the influence of family, friends, and colleagues and all they have shared with me and taught me over the years. I strongly believe we are all here to become better people through learning how to take care of and help each other. To that end, it is no surprise that my list of acknowledgments is lengthy.

While my name is on the cover of this book, there are dozens of people who have been vitally important in bringing this book to the world. First and foremost, I would like to thank Ellen W. Stiefler, who believed in the important mission of this book from the onset. Her encouragement and endless sound advice have made this book possible. I couldn't be more grateful.

Ellen Reid poured her talent into this book and brought together an exceptional literary team. This book would not be possible without her unwavering support and vision. My thanks go to Patricia Bacall and Laren Bright for their many contributions.

I would like to thank Annette Wick, friend and fellow writer, who convinced me to continue on with this message despite raising my own three children and working outside the home. Her support and practical advice kept this project moving forward.

My colleague and friend, Kate Merrilees, has taught me nearly everything I know about the world of infants and toddlers. Watching her treat each and every parent, child, and professional with complete respect and kindness has profoundly affected me. Likewise, I am indebted to Lynne Reckman, whose careful reading of this manuscript and suggestions have made the voice of infants and toddlers heard better through my words.

I would like to thank Tracy Cook, ProKids Executive Director, for her encouragement and support throughout this project, as well as her suggestions for making the book the best it could be. Additionally, Charlotte Caples, ProKids CASA Program Director, mentored me on how to be a true advocate for children. She became the role model I needed as a young professional.

I deeply appreciate the input from Mark Piepmeier, Hamilton County Assistant Prosecutor, and Senator Tom Niehaus, whose contributions have added depth and value to the pages of this book.

All my co-workers at ProKids work tirelessly everyday on behalf of children. I have learned so much from them over the years, and enjoyed the benefit of their knowledge, not to mention their sense of humor. Their dedication to children is astounding and an honor to witness.

I am honored to work alongside ProKids CASAs. I'm humbled and awed by their never-ending passion and contributions to children.

Countless families have crossed my path over the past fifteen years, and each has taught me something. For that I am grateful, especially for the children. This book would not exist if not for them.

My mother, Hanna Eck, nourished in me, from an early age, the importance of helping others and making the world a better place. My five siblings have had a significant influence on me as I have grown, and I appreciate all of them. Gretchen Eck has supplied many coffee time-outs and a constant faith in my abilities. Barb Rengering has always stood ready to help me in any way possible, even when I don't ask for it. She is my biggest cheerleader. My aunts, Mary Patricia and Dorothea, have supported this book entirely. My mother-in-law, Dolores Schlaack, has given my entire family the incredible gift of her time and love. Having her care for my children while I work has been a tremendous blessing. I can never thank her enough.

My former teacher, friend, and spiritual mentor, Father Larry Tensi, encouraged me for two decades to write a book that would maybe help make the world a better place. His steadfast belief in my abilities has enabled me to succeed. I'm grateful for his constant presence in my life.

Most of all, my gratitude goes to my husband, Ed, and our children, Hanna, Grace, and Ben. This book has been the other individual in our house over the past year, and they have accepted it and encouraged it, while inspiring me with their ability to let me know when it was time to put the book away and enjoy our time together. I love each of them more than they could ever know and I thank them for the opportunity to be a wife and a mother, the two most important roles in my life.

PREFACE

WHEN HISTORICAL EVENTS OCCUR, people often can tell you where they were and what they were doing when they heard the news. My mother remembers being in the parking garage of a department store when she learned President Kennedy had been shot. I was wiping down lunch tables in my grade school cafeteria when I overheard one teacher tell another that the spaceship Challenger had fallen from the sky. On 9/11, I was circling a city block in downtown Cincinnati, running late for court and trying to score a parking meter, when a frantic voice over the radio reported seeing the second tower get hit.

These are the before and after moments of our lives that we share with our fellow Americans. They are defining. In addition, we all have private before and after moments. In my life's list of before and after moments, I vividly recall those related to Marcus Fiesel. The phone rang and I grabbed it while emptying a hamper of clothes into a laundry basket. A co-worker was on the line.

"Did you hear about the three-year-old boy missing in the park?" she asked.

My heart skipped a beat. I looked up to see my youngest son, Ben, newly four and playing with the toy dinosaurs he had received as birthday gifts a week earlier. The horror of losing a child, I thought.

My co-worker continued. "Holly, he's a foster child." My heart dropped to the floor while I stood sorting whites and darks.

"What's his name?" I asked. Relief washed over me as I learned it was not a child I knew. The second question flew from my lips. "Who are his foster parents?" I searched my memory for some recollection of Liz and David Carroll, but none came to mind.

My days are full of young foster children like Marcus Fiesel. As a Guardian Ad Litem (GAL) in Hamilton County Juvenile Court, my job is to represent the best interests of children who have been abused or neglected by their parents. I work for ProKids CASA Program, a non-profit agency dedicated to ensuring safe, permanent, and nurturing homes for children. My caseload involves abused and neglected infants and toddlers. As a ProKids GAL, I work alongside community volunteers known as CASAs (Court Appointed Special Advocates). Together we learn as much as possible about the children assigned to us and make recommendations to a juvenile court magistrate or judge about what is in their best interest.

On the night I learned this little foster boy was missing, I went to bed, but didn't sleep. I tossed and turned while the statistics about young foster children roared in my head. More likely to be abused and neglected than children in the general population. More likely to be abused and neglected than older children. 77% of all homicide victims are under the age of four (US Department of Health and Human Services, 2006). More likely to suffer a horrendous fate…

For the next two weeks, Marcus' picture dominated the news. Two thousand people searched for him in the park, in the woods, and in neighboring communities. The blue-eyed, brown-haired little boy who vanished riveted the entire community.

In the thirteen long days after Marcus was reported missing, my CASAs and I visited all of the young children we represented. I was driving home from one such visit when breaking news interrupted the music streaming from my car radio. A press conference was airing. In it, Hamilton County Prosecutor Joe Deters revealed that charges were being brought against Marcus' foster parents in connection with his murder. Again, my heart felt like it dropped from my chest and fell to the ground.

Before Marcus, his community knew little about foster children and the vulnerabilities they face. Before Marcus, we assumed that children like him were not our responsibility, but instead the responsibility of Children's Services. Before Marcus, people were lulled into the misconception that children in foster care are safe and protected from others who harm them. Before Marcus, children like him were largely unseen by the community as a whole.

Marcus' story cannot end with his death, the life snuffed out of him early and brutally. His story must continue on in our commitment to abused and neglected children who walk in this world among us. Marcus put a face on the foster children who live in the shadows of our lives, unseen. They rely on us to reach out and give them a hand into a world that is safe, kind, and loving.

Invisible Kids invites readers to learn more about foster children and empowers them to take positive action, creating change for the half million children just like Marcus who belong to a government system instead of a loving family. Before Marcus, vulnerable young foster children were invisible to the community around them.

The After Marcus is up to you.

CHAPTER 1

Little Marcus

IVE-YEAR-OLD JOEY LEANED ACROSS the kitchen table, his brown eyes as dark as night, and whispered, "Do you know about the little boy who died in the closet?"

"Yes. I know about that little boy. How do you know about him?" I asked.

Joey's eyes remained fixed on mine. "My mom told me about him. She said if I told anyone her boyfriend was living here, then I would have to go to foster care. Then they would tape me up, lock me in the closet, and kill me."

"You must have been very scared when the police and the social worker came to take you to a foster home," I replied.

Sensing I was interested in hearing all he had to say, those big brown eyes swam with tears. His voice quivered, "I was crying half to death when I got here." His words tumbled out faster and faster as he dumped his terror onto the kitchen table in front of me. "I thought I was going to die. I haven't seen my baby brother. Do you know where they took him? Is he dead?"

Joey had been living in foster care for only a few days when I first met him. As a Guardian Ad Litem appointed through Hamilton County Juvenile Court in Cincinnati, Ohio it is my job to represent the best interests of children who have been abused or neglected. I was appointed to represent Joey and his six-month-old brother, Jordan, after a Children's Services caseworker filed a motion in court seeking the boys' placement in foster care. I met the boys' mother, and her boyfriend, in court the morning after the boys were placed in an emergency foster home.

I sat through hours of testimony from the caseworker, the police officer, and finally, the mother herself. Through their testimony, it became clear that Joey's mother had been using drugs for several years. The police had been called to their home repeatedly for domestic disturbances. In the latest incident, Joey had jumped in front of his mother to protect her from her enraged boyfriend. He had been shoved to the side and fell to the ground. The police responded to a neighbor's 911 call. Joey and his brother were placed in foster care. Now the court would decide what should happen.

The juvenile court magistrate counted on me to learn as much as possible about the boys and their lives. This information would determine what kind of help Joey and Jordan needed while they lived in foster care, and where they would ultimately reside. The court also relied on me to ensure that the boys were safe and well cared for during this time.

Sitting through testimony, and hearing all the horrific details about children like Joey and Jordan's troubled lives, is common in my line of work. What I was not prepared for were those terrified brown eyes, convinced that placement in foster care was a death sentence. The highly publicized story of murdered foster child Marcus Fiesel had been rippling through the communities near where he lived. County agencies and the courts were re-examining foster care practices and politicians were introducing new laws to protect foster children. But I had no idea this ripple effect would make its way into the hearts of little boys like Joey and be used to terrify them into silence.

Joey knew about Marcus Fiesel and the brutal death he suffered at the hands of his foster parents. Marcus became a household name in Southwestern Ohio during the summer of 2006. Three-year-old Marcus, abused, neglected, and suffering from developmental delays, had been placed in foster care after his mother, Donna Trevino, could no longer care for him. Marcus had been living with his foster parents, David and Liz Carroll, for a little more than three months when his foster mother reported him missing in a neighborhood park. His picture was plastered across TV screens and newspapers throughout the region. He looked into the camera, his chubby little hands held up in front of his mouth, as if he was trying to contain the wonder and joy of discovering all that this world had to offer. His mischievous grin lit his face against the backdrop of a green blanket of grass. This picture of Marcus remained in the public eye from the time he was reported missing until the conclusion of his foster parents' murder trial.

In life, Marcus endured physical abuse and neglect and was placed in foster care for his protection. He was a three-year-old foster child who was invisible to the community around him, shuffled from home to home like unwanted inventory. In death, Marcus struggled for his last gasps of air in a small closet that registered between 105 and 110 degrees after his foster parents bound him in a blanket and wrapped him in packing tape for two days in the August heat. The helplessness he faced in life was matched only by the power of his story to put a face on the thousands of young foster children who journey through their childhoods belonging to a system rather than with a loving family.

While Joey's mom used Marcus' story to scare her son into silence, many others used Marcus' life and death to examine the foster care system and seek ways to improve the lives of other abused and neglected children. Young children like Marcus are especially vulnerable when they are abused and neglected by the people who should protect them instinctively. Subsequent placement in foster care does not guarantee an end to their suffering. I've learned many things over the years spanning my career as a Guardian Ad Litem in Hamilton County Juvenile Court. I've represented the best interests of hundreds of abused and neglected infants and toddlers. Immersed in their world and in their language, one thing was always crystal clear when nothing else seemed cut and dry: the vulnerabilities they face are shocking.

Universally, the foster care system is intended to offer sanctuary to children like Marcus who have been abused or neglected so severely that they are taken away from their parents. In reality, children in foster care are ten times more likely to be abused than children in the general population (Maier, 1997) and nearly twice as likely to die of abuse in foster care (U. S. Department of Health and Human Services, 2002). Despite the safeguards in place to ensure quality care for every child placed in foster care, not every foster home is safe. Tragically for Marcus, he landed in the hands of foster parents who would take his life.

On the same day Marcus was placed in the home of Liz and David Carroll, a two-year-old girl named Callie was placed in a different foster home. Callie's mother was mentally ill and homeless. She was not taking her prescribed medication and was hearing voices telling her to hurt Callie. A neighbor who lived in the apartment next door called Children's Services when she heard Callie crying and her mother screaming. A Children's Services caseworker visited the home and found the little girl with a black eye. The caseworker determined that Callie was at great risk of further abuse or neglect if she remained in the care of her mother. The court intervened and Callie was placed in foster care. Like Marcus, Callie was placed in a home with a foster mother and father and their older children. Severely withdrawn, Callie preferred to be left alone rather than interact with the family around her. Determined to save this little girl, her foster parents sought advice and help from a therapist who was skilled in helping young children like Callie develop healthy relationships with significant adult figures.

On the day Marcus was reported missing, Callie was helping her foster mother harvest vegetables from their garden. Callie blossomed under the care and love of this family. When her biological mother committed suicide by a drug overdose, and no other family member could raise her, Callie's foster parents decided to adopt her. At the time of Marcus' funeral, nine months after his death, Callie's adoption was in its final process. When Marcus' remains were buried, Callie was happy and thriving with her family. How is this possible?

The risk of maltreatment remains when a bureaucracy becomes responsible for the care and safety of a young child. In a game of chance, professionals work to ensure the protection of all foster children. Laws that govern the licensing of foster parents and the care of foster children provided the framework of Marcus' care. An army of professionals became responsible for Marcus when his family failed him. Each held a piece to the puzzle of his life. His foster parents held the largest piece of all. Tragically, these pieces never came together to create a picture of a happy childhood for Marcus. Callie's foster parents also held the largest piece of the puzzle of Callie's life. From the time she met them, the pieces all fell into place. For Callie, the system worked. For Marcus, the system failed miserably.

Imagine for a moment that you are new in town and seeking a doctor to provide you and your family routine medical care. You choose a doctor who's close to your house, thinking the convenience of this location was a high priority. You arrive for your new patient visit and sign in. You are kept waiting for over an hour and when you finally meet your new doctor you notice his gruff demeanor and questionable hygiene. He looks over your paperwork and asks a couple of questions. You have several for him, but he does not seem to welcome them. You mention concerns about ongoing headaches, and he implies that the stress of your move must be the root of the problem and not to worry. You leave his office feeling uneasy about putting your medical care in his hands.

Now, imagine a different scenario. You arrive at your new doctor's office and are impressed by the genuine care emanating from the receptionist who signs you in. Your name is called within minutes. Your new doctor enters the room, smiles, shakes your hand, and introduces himself. He is intent on hearing about your medical history and your current concerns. He asks many questions about the headaches you have been having, and thoughtfully offers suggestions, possible treatments, or medical tests that could be performed. He actively encourages you to be his partner in your medical care. You leave his office with a plan of action regarding your headaches and feel confident that you are in good hands.

Both doctors are licensed practitioners. Both went to medical school. Both passed the state boards and both have medical practices. However, the care and service they provide to their patients are not the same. This is true for nearly every profession. There are good doctors and bad doctors, good teachers and bad teachers. Some have even perpetrated crimes, sexual or otherwise, against the people entrusted to their care. Foster parents are no different. Background checks and required training go a long way in ensuring the safety and care of children. Unfortunately, there are no guarantees that every foster parent is committed to caring for the children placed in their home.

If you do not like your new doctor, you have the ability to leave and find a new one. Foster children don't choose their home and can't choose to leave. Young foster children are at an even greater disadvantage. They can't communicate with words what is happening behind the closed door of a foster home. They do not go to school where a teacher observes them for hours each day. Often, days, weeks, and sometimes even months pass without these young children being seen or heard by the professionals responsible for overseeing their care.

Caseworkers who place children in foster care must accept the homes that are available. That may include a foster home where there has been suspected, but unsubstantiated, abuse of children. When a child needs a foster home, she doesn't have the luxury of waiting for the right one to come along. Furthermore, there are never enough good foster homes for the children who need them. Caseworkers rarely have the option of several choices. Foster children are placed in homes that have space. Oftentimes, caseworkers placing children are simply given a name and address of where to deliver them.

Foster care is essentially a service created to meet a need. Government funded Children's Services provides children with a place to live and pays people who are willing to take care of them. Foster care agencies are created to recruit, train, and oversee foster parents and their homes. Ideally, foster care agencies take government money and put the bulk of it into supporting quality foster homes and services for children. Unfortunately, some of these agencies take shortcuts on training and monitoring foster parents, and instead, beef up the salaries of their CEO and other employees.

Little Marcus was not yet three years old when he was found wandering the streets alone in April 2006. A passerby called the police, and they responded along with a Children's Services caseworker. They determined that Marcus could not be safe while in the care of his mother. His father was not involved in his life, and there were no other relatives willing or able to take care of him. Foster care was necessary. For this reason, the caseworker sought the court's intervention. As a result, interim custody of Marcus was granted to the Butler County Children's Services Board. Once this happened, Marcus' caseworker set about finding a foster home willing to take him.

In searching for a foster home that would accept Marcus, his caseworker turned to a private foster care agency named Lifeway for Youth. Lifeway for Youth is a non-profit agency that recruits and trains people to become qualified treatment foster parents (also referred to as therapeutic foster parents) for special needs children. These special needs children may suffer from medical, behavioral, or emotional problems and are generally thought to be more challenging than other children. After Lifeway built a pool of treatment foster families, it contracted with children's services agencies to provide foster homes for abused and neglected children. Children's Services often has their own pool of foster parents. When a foster family cannot be located within the Children's Services system, a foster home is sought through a private agency.

The Ohio Administrative Code, Chapter 5101:2-7 outlines requirements for foster homes. Twenty pages of regulations detail the rules and requirements for foster homes, down to the space permitted between crib slats.

Just like physicians attend medical school and eventually take state board exams before they are licensed, prospective foster parents must also undergo certain requirements prior to being licensed. The goal of this comprehensive process is to ensure that foster parents will provide quality care to children.

The process is lengthy and involved. A thorough reading of the law as it relates to foster parent licensure could lead a person to believe it is impossible to license a substandard home. The process of licensing prospective foster parents involves investigating the applicants and their home, as well as providing training to them, and later monitoring them after a license is granted.

Potential foster parents are required to undergo criminal background checks and fingerprinting. They also undergo a medical examination by a licensed physician and provide documentation verifying they are in good health. Candidates submit three references from non-family sources to vouch for them. They must disclose the names and ages of all individuals living in their home. Background checks on these people, if they are older than eighteen, are also required.

Social workers from children's services agencies or private foster care agencies inspect potential foster homes to assess cleanliness, adequate repair, and space for foster children. As part of the home investigation, family finances are examined. Potential foster parents must prove there is sufficient income to meet the needs of their family without reimbursement for foster care. The family's income and employment history are verified through pay stubs and contact with employers.

Additionally, candidates must complete training before they can be licensed. The number of hours required varies from state to state. If potential foster parents seek a license to care for special needs children, they must complete more training than foster parents who do not plan to house children who have serious medical or behavioral problems. This training may include topics related to special needs children and how to effectively parent them.

In the process of obtaining a license to practice medicine, resident doctors work in hospitals or other clinical settings. Senior doctors evaluate them during this time. Similarly, Lifeway for Youth evaluated Liz and David Carroll during the time they were working toward obtaining their foster care license. Lifeway was responsible for overseeing every aspect of the Carrolls' application to become foster parents. They reported that Liz and David attended thirty-six hours of training. A home visit, fire inspection, and safety audit were completed in November and December of 2005. Lifeway assured the Ohio Department of Job and Family Services that the Carrolls had successfully completed all requirements necessary to be licensed foster parents.

The Ohio Department of Job and Family Services issued a foster care license, allowing up to four foster children to be placed with the Carrolls, and then the Carrolls were added to the list of foster homes available through Lifeway for Youth.

Prior to Marcus' placement with Liz and David Carroll, a team of professionals met to discuss his needs and potential placement in the Carrolls' foster home. These professionals included Marcus' Butler County Children's Services caseworker and an administrator from that office. The team also included three staff members from Lifeway and a representative from an agency that serves children with developmental delays.

Finding a foster home for Marcus was more difficult because of his developmental delays and high energy level. Reports suggested he was autistic, and that he had a history of smearing his feces. He was also undergoing diagnostic testing that required that his foster parents take him to and from these additional medical appointments. It would take a committed family to care for Marcus. That Liz was not employed outside the home was likely seen as a bonus for Marcus, as he would not need to make additional transitions to a childcare setting.

After a thorough discussion about Marcus and his needs, the team recommended placement with the Carrolls. Marcus' Butler County Children's Services caseworker accepted this placement.

On May 5, 2006, one month prior to his third birthday, Marcus was delivered to the doorstep of David and Liz Carroll's home. Unbeknownst to the Children's Services and Lifeway caseworkers, family dynamics in the Carrolls' home had changed.

Although David and Liz led caseworkers to believe they were a happily married couple raising four children, more was happening behind closed doors. David and Liz had opened their home to their live-in girlfriend, Amy Baker, and her three children. Marcus' foster home was much more crowded at this point. Three adults lived in the home, in addition to the seven children between them. Another foster child lived there also, totaling eight children. Marcus was the ninth.

In early August 2006, the Carrolls planned a weekend trip to Williamstown, Kentucky, for a family reunion with Liz's relatives. The Carrolls could have called Lifeway for Youth and requested respite care for Marcus so that he could stay with another foster family while they were away. In fact, they had used respite care twice during the weeks Marcus lived with them. They chose not to access respite care for this trip. Amy Baker later testified that they did not access respite care and did not want to take Marcus with them to the family reunion to face questions about a bruise. David had left Marcus sleeping in his car seat one night, leaving a large bruise on his neck.

Liz and David decided to leave the toddler behind. Together, they took Marcus' arms and pinned them behind his back. They wrapped him in a blanket and then wrapped clear packing tape around the blanket, ensuring he could not get free. They left him on the floor of a bedroom closet. Amy Baker watched all this and suggested that they at least put him in a playpen so he would be more comfortable. They placed him in the playpen in the closet, switched on a small fan, and shut the door behind them. It was nearly 90 degrees that day.

Amy, David, Liz, and their children piled into the family's GMC Envoy to leave for Kentucky. Liz ran back into the house to retrieve something. Amy Baker later testified that when Liz returned to the SUV, she said, "He's freaking out."

They backed out of the driveway and headed out of town.

He's freaking out. Stop for a minute. Think about the sheer terror Marcus must have felt. Close your eyes, put your arms behind your back, and imagine you cannot move. Imagine sweat forming on your brow and trickling slowly down your face. You can't even reach up to brush it away. The blanket, the prison that will snuff the life out of your body, soaks up your sweat. Seconds turn into minutes, minutes into hours. No one comes. *He's freaking out.*

Hamilton County Coroner, O'Dell Owens, later speculated that Marcus died from heat exhaustion. He was likely bound in the oppressive, broiling closet for twenty-four hours before he died. Given the outside temperature, the temperature inside the closet could have easily topped 110 degrees (Coolidge, 2006). With little air circulating, Marcus' last, desperate gasps likely would have left his little nostrils burning.

While Marcus was enduring this long agony, Amy, David, Liz, and their children checked into a hotel in Kentucky. They checked out the next morning and attended the family reunion. They camped on Saturday night with relatives.

Around three a.m. Sunday, David awoke and insisted they return to home to check on Marcus. They gathered their children, and piled into the family SUV for the trip home. They arrived home around 6 a.m. David ran upstairs for Marcus.

He was dead.

Amy Baker testified that David screamed when he found Marcus' little body, stiff and hard, blood had trickled from his nose. His little toes were rubbed raw, likely from struggling to break free from the playpen, rubbing his feet against the mesh. David placed Marcus' body in a large cardboard box, threw clothes over it, and then carried it out of the house. David and Amy climbed into the car with the cardboard box and drove to a nearby gas station. Footage from a security camera at the station revealed that they bought two gas cans and filled them with gas. At Amy's suggestion, they drove to rural Brown County, their destination being an old, abandoned chimney. This isolated chimney was all that remained of an old home vacated decades ago. Two stories in height, it left just enough space at the base to dump and burn a small body. They doused Marcus' body with gasoline, set it afire and waited for it to burn. It did not.

They doused it again, set it on fire and waited, then again. When Marcus' body failed to burn entirely, they gathered the remains into two pillowcases, drove to the Ohio River, and dumped them in the water.

Back at the house, Liz was caring for the other children. Amy Baker testified that Liz had put a teddy bear in Marcus' bed, and told the children that Marcus was in his room. Over the next ten days, Liz or David told the other children that Marcus was with his biological mother, or in school.

On August 10, Marcus' caseworker arrived for her weekly, scheduled visit at the Carrolls' home. Liz invited her inside and they sat at the kitchen table discussing Marcus' progress and upcoming MRI, which was scheduled at Cincinnati Children's Hospital in the upcoming weeks. Liz looked tired and reported that Marcus had been up ill all night. Not wanting to disturb a sick child, the caseworker left the home without seeing him. According to Lifeway for Youth, Liz neither encouraged nor discouraged the caseworker from seeing him.

Days passed and the Carrolls were running out of time. Marcus' appointment at the Women, Infants and Children (WIC) Office was scheduled for the afternoon of August 15, 2006. That morning, Liz and David staged Marcus' disappearance. Liz went to a park with two of her children, a foster child and a little girl she was babysitting. She feigned a fainting spell and reported that when she came to, Marcus was gone.

When the police responded to the park and took the report of a missing child, they immediately set about looking for him, while simultaneously determining whether foul play had occurred. Although Liz had reportedly fainted, she did not suffer any bruises or scratches to her face that would have been common under such circumstances. The police got permission to search the Carrolls' home. What they found was disturbing.

The home was reportedly messy and cluttered. Of more concern, however, were the numerous holes that had been punched in the walls. Liz told police that David's anger was responsible for the holes. Further investigation revealed that police had visited the home less than two months earlier. They had responded to a domestic violence altercation between David and Liz.

As Liz and David's story of Marcus missing in the park began to unravel, so did the facts surrounding Lifeway for Youth's recommendation of them as foster parents. Three months after Marcus' death, the Ohio Department of Job and Family Services (ODJFS) released a report detailing their investigation of Lifeway for Youth's activities surrounding their recommendation of the Carrolls as therapeutic foster parents. They found a number of violations.

According to ODJFS, the home study completed on Liz and David Carroll did not contain the required information regarding the foster parents' marriage and relationship, medical conditions, the foster father's children, the Carrolls' attitudes regarding methods of discipline, complete work histories, and information regarding the daycare Liz ran out of their home. The Carrolls provided three references, one of whom was a relative, another was from Amy Baker. Lifeway did not contact any of the references (Ohio Department of Job and Family Services, 2006).

Lifeway also over-reported the number of foster caregiver training hours the agency provided. As a result, the Carrolls were recommended for certification prior to completing the required amount of pre-service training (Ohio Department of Job and Family Services, 2006). It doesn't stop there. ODJFS found that Lifeway did not document that the foster parents met the experience, education, and training requirements necessary to be certified as treatment foster parents (Ohio Department of Job and Family Services, 2006).

Relative to Marcus' placement, home visits conducted by Lifeway did not meet the required frequency standards. Meetings with the professionals involved with Marcus were not held regularly and a plan for respite care for him was not developed. The treatment plans on file for Marcus were not co-signed by a supervisor as required, and the supervisor lacked the professional license required to act in this capacity (Ohio Department of Job and Family Services, 2006).

Within a week of Marcus' arrival at the Carrolls' home, he was visited by a social worker from Lifeway as well as his Butler County Children's Services caseworker. It is not uncommon for a Children's Services caseworker to feel a sense of relief after placing a behaviorally challenging child in a therapeutic foster home. Once a child is placed in a network like Lifeway, a social worker from that agency joins the team and helps monitor the home.

As a former Children's Services caseworker, I placed seven-year-old Jamie in a therapeutic foster home. I was grateful for the extra set of eyes on her. I felt like I could step back and attend more to my other cases where children were at far greater risk. After all, the network caseworker was visiting Jamie every week and making sure she was supported in her placement. Imagine my shock and horror when I received a call two weeks later from Jamie's teacher. Her teacher was calling to report that Jamie was coming to school dirty and hungry. The lesson of that experience stayed with me long after Jamie's case ended. Make no assumptions.

Marcus' caseworker through Lifeway was responsible for monitoring Marcus' placement in the Carrolls' home. When she received Marcus' case, she would likely have operated under the assumption that because the Carrolls had been licensed, they were safe and appropriate to care for Marcus. They lived in a spacious two-story, five-bedroom home. The home had completed a fire inspection and a safety audit. The caseworker didn't know it was rented, and not owned as they reported in the process of being licensed.

During the licensing process, the Carrolls' finances should have been investigated. They had reported that David Carroll worked for eight years at the same job. They also reported Liz Carroll received income as a licensed daycare provider. This would explain the number of children in the home when the caseworker visited. Lifeway reported that the Carrolls met all requirements to become foster parents, and as a result, the state issued a foster care license. Neither Marcus' county caseworker nor his Lifeway caseworker was responsible for ensuring the license was appropriately issued. That duty belonged to the administration at Lifeway. As circumstances unfolded, it became clear that Liz and David Carroll should never have been licensed.

Lifeway assured Marcus' Butler County caseworker that a foster family existed who could meet all of his needs. When the Butler County caseworker accepted Marcus' placement with the Carrolls, the Butler County Children's Services Board agreed to pay Lifeway a daily fee to care for Marcus. This rate was negotiated between the Butler County Administration and Lifeway for Youth's Administration. Lifeway would then keep half the money and give the other half to the Carrolls. The Carrolls received a board rate of $33.50 per day or roughly $1000 per month. Believing the Carrolls had sufficient income to meet the needs of all the children in their home, the Lifeway caseworker probably never suspected that they were relying on the board rate they received for Marcus to pay their bills.

The caseworker's primary role was to ensure Marcus' needs were met. Her secondary role was to support the Carrolls as foster parents. Foster homes are scarce. It is important to support foster parents in their role so they will continue fostering children. The Carrolls had a vested interest in appearing as though Marcus was thriving in their home. They would likely talk a good game about how his behavior had improved and how he was progressing developmentally. This didn't stop Liz from requesting additional money from Lifeway. She asked her Lifeway caseworker if Marcus could be considered medically fragile, which would increase the board rate to $50 per day. Lifeway refused. With Marcus' limited ability to communicate and the lack of other professionals laying eyes on him daily, there was nothing to contradict what the Carrolls were reporting.

Amy Baker testified to facts regarding Marcus' death in the closet, the burning of his body, and his burial in the river. As disturbing as it was to hear those details, my heart ached over her description of Marcus' daily life in the foster home that was supposed to be his sanctuary from abuse and neglect. Amy described how nobody ever did anything with him. The toddler stayed in his room most of the time. He was bathed, fed, and left alone.

What would it be like to wander, day after day on your own as a toddler without anyone loving you, wrapping you in his or her arms and showering you with tenderness? What would it be like to get a bath or food, and nothing more?

A toddler's days are supposed to be filled with hugs and kisses, nursery rhymes and storybooks. They are supposed to be filled with giggles, swings, and ladybugs. Marcus never knew those days. *He's freaking out.*

At the time of Marcus' death, I had been appointed to represent the best interests of about sixty infants and toddlers who had been abused or neglected and were under the jurisdiction of the neighboring Hamilton County Juvenile

Court. Nearly twenty-five of these little ones lived in Lifeway foster homes. County and Lifeway caseworkers and I double and triple checked all of these homes. Even so, I was haunted by the fact that I may have missed something.

Being assigned to represent these other children during the media storm around Marcus was not unlike lying in bed trying to determine whether danger lurked in my house. Were the foster parents I visited during the day as invested in their charges as they seemed, or were they putting on a show for me? Was a two-year-old's temper tantrum simply that, or was it some kind of cry for help? Which homes could be trusted and which could not?

My own fears and sense of helplessness were matched not only by my co-workers' and other system professionals' at the time, but also by the thousands of people who lived in the region. Marcus' story hit all of our hearts. News traveled fast when Marcus was reported missing in the park. The community had been called to join in the search. Motivated to save this little boy's life, people turned out in droves to scour the park and nearby woods, determined to bring him to safety. They combed every inch of the park, desperate to rescue him. They played music, hoping to entice him out of his hiding place. Two days later, when police officially called off their search, dozens of volunteers continued looking, not wanting to give up hope that Marcus would be found unharmed. In reality, Marcus had been dead for ten days.

People were invested in saving Marcus from the danger that lurked in the woods. They searched for him, prayed for him, and money was offered for his safe return. In the days following his alleged disappearance, Marcus became a name and face known to virtually everyone. He became the community's child. Not surprisingly, his community was devastated to learn that their little boy had suffered such a horrendous death at the hands of a foster care system intended to save his life.

Marcus Fiesel's death rippled through the foster care system in a variety of ways, one of which was to frighten the children placed in foster homes. Five-year-old Joey was horrified when he went to foster care; he was convinced that he would suffer the same fate as Marcus Fiesel. Prior to his foster care placement, Joey experienced severe physical abuse and witnessed chronic domestic violence between his mother and her boyfriend. He was terrified and separated from his baby brother. Being removed from his mother did not make him feel rescued. Instead, he believed it would kill him.

The pain and fear in Joey's eyes as he recounted to me the night he left his mother's home were unmatched by any I had ever seen. He was visibly relieved when I told him I had just visited his baby brother before I came to see him. Jordan was fine. I told Joey that Jordan had been wearing pajamas with baseballs on them, and that he was having his last bottle before he went to sleep. I told him that Jordan's foster parents were very nice people. I assured him that soon he would be able to visit with his brother. I also assured Joey that he was not going to die in a closet. I told him that his caseworker and I would make sure he was OK, and his foster parents were here to help him and keep him safe. As I left Joey's foster home, I thought long and hard about him and how he feared for his life.

He's freaking out.

I thought about how the system failed Marcus and many children before him. Surely, it would fail again. I thought about the thousands of people who searched for Marcus, prayed for him, and wept over his tragic life and death. These ordinary citizens felt the devastation of Marcus' death, and they were also the best hope of other young foster children. They could make a difference for the hundreds of foster children who live in Marcus' community.

Marcus Fiesel's family failed him. The foster care system failed him. The community failed him. But a half a million foster children like Marcus are still here across America, waiting to be given a chance at a childhood.

We can't fail them.

CHAPTER 2

From Broken Home to Broken System

OR MARCUS, THE HORRIFIC end of his life was the exclamation point at the end of a terrible sentence. Abuse and neglect routinely punctuated his short life; first by his family and later by the system and people entrusted to care for him.

Like many young foster children, Marcus Fiesel arrived in this world with the deck stacked against him. He was born into poverty to a single mother, who could barely manage the task of caring for his older brother, let alone a newborn. His father was not involved in his life, leaving his mother to be the sole provider for all his needs. Marcus' mother was a product of the foster care system, having been abused and neglected as a child.

Children's Services caseworkers first met Marcus when he was one year old after an allegation of neglect. His family's home was flea-infested, dirty, and reeked of mold and feces (*Cincinnati Enquirer*, September 3, 2006). Like the parents of many other foster children, Marcus' mother was in a relationship with a violent man. Despite the fleas and the filth, the greatest risk posed to Marcus was the violence occurring between his mother and her boyfriend.

The results are disastrous when children live in the midst of domestic violence. Living in a state of perpetual fear has toxic effects on a young child's developing brain, impacting everything from cognitive development to emotional well-being. Additionally, children exposed to domestic violence are much more likely to be physically abused. "There is significant overlap between domestic violence and child abuse—in families where one form of violence exists, it is likely the other does too" (National Council of Juvenile and Family Court Judges, 1999). At just a year old, Marcus' future looked darker than the bruises that were on his horizon.

A year later, in September 2005, a Children's Services caseworker investigated an allegation of physical abuse against Marcus. He was barely two years old. Marcus had a bruise on his buttocks after allegedly being beaten by his mother's boyfriend. Marcus and his brother, Michael, were placed in foster care.

One month later, a juvenile court magistrate ruled that Marcus and Michael could be safely returned to their mother after Donna promised to change her lifestyle. Marcus had not lived with his mother for long when he climbed out of a two-story window and toppled to the ground, requiring stitches to his chin. A detective investigated this January 2006 incident and reported that Marcus was a handful; into everything so much that his mother was exhausted just trying to keep up with him. He was always moving. With Marcus, there was never any down time. He required constant supervision.

In April 2006, Marcus' case appeared again in juvenile court after he was found wandering on a busy street and was nearly hit by a car. A caseworker investigated this allegation of neglect. As the allegations and investigations piled up over time, it became clearer to the caseworkers, and later to the court, that Marcus simply could not be safe while in the care of his mother. When confronted with the painful reality that children's services would petition again the court to have her children removed from her, Donna willingly gave up custody of Marcus, Michael, and their baby sister, Peaches. This triggered the children's placement in foster care. Every day across America, siblings are taken from their parents, and ripped from each other as well. There are far too few foster homes available to accommodate sibling sets. Foster homes have a bed here, a bed there, but not always three beds together. This was the reality for Marcus and his siblings. They lost each other when they were placed in separate foster homes. Marcus started his final journey into foster care, just two months shy of his third birthday.

When he was born, Marcus was placed in the hands of his mother. It was her responsibility to love him, care for him, and protect him with her life. When she failed him, no other family or friends came forward to help him. Marcus was forced to rely on a government system for protection, to do the job of his parents.

Economists warn us that we can't depend on social security benefits to fund our retirement, even if as adults we have paid into the system all our working lives. We cannot rely on the government to take care of us in our old age. Yet foster children are forced to rely on this same government to sustain, guide, and nurture them if they are not fortunate enough to find safety within their own family. When children are placed in the hands of the government for protection and oversight, they often slip through the fingers of the multitude of people charged with caring for them. It should come as no surprise that the government often fails miserably when it is forced to take on the role of overseeing the growth and development of children. People working within the foster care system recognize that it is far from perfect. However, it is necessary. Physical abuse, neglect, and trauma have generally been present with some consistency in the lives of children when they are made subjects of court complaints.

Foster children are the subjects of child protection cases. These cases are heard in juvenile court by a magistrate or judge. In some cities across America, judges preside over child protection cases. In larger cities, there are too many cases and not enough judges to hear them all, so the judges appoint magistrates to hear the cases instead. Marcus' caseworker made the recommendation for him to be placed in foster care. A juvenile court magistrate heard evidence from the caseworker and made the decision regarding what was in Marcus' best interest according to the law.

A judge or magistrate makes important decisions about children only after all legal parties present their case to him or her. The legal parties and their representatives involved in these cases include a Children's Services caseworker along with his or her attorney, who is a prosecutor assigned to child protection cases for the county. Other legal parties include the biological parents, and if parents have separate interests, they each have their own attorney. If they cannot afford attorneys, they are represented by public defenders. These public defenders are available on the first day a case is heard in court. Each of these people has a hand in influencing the decisions made by a judge or magistrate.

Every child alleged to be abused or neglected is required to have a Guardian Ad Litem appointed to represent him or her. GALs are also legal parties to the proceedings. Guardian Ad Litem is Latin meaning "Guardian in the meantime." This person does not act as a legal guardian to the child, provide a home, or have custody. Instead, this person's role is to represent the best interests of the child while the court is involved in a case. The GAL is the one professional involved in the case whose only focus is on what's best for the child. The county caseworker works with the entire family. The parents and their attorney focus on the wishes of the parents. The judge or magistrate is forced to juggle the legal interests of the parties and make decisions based on the law.

Although the Children's Services caseworker plays an important role in monitoring foster children, he or she is not the only professional playing an active role in the life of a foster child. The GAL attends all court hearings regarding children and makes recommendations to the judge about what is best for them. In order to do this effectively, the GAL conducts an independent investigation separate from the Children's Services caseworker. This includes attending home visits and meetings related to children, such as school meetings. The GAL participates in all decisions regarding children including placement, therapeutic or educational services, and services for parents who are attempting to reunify. The GAL is also involved in all decisions regarding family visitation, including the frequency, duration, and whether visits are supervised.

The role of a GAL is vital to the court process as an independent voice for children's best interests. The downside is that GALs typically have caseloads much higher than Children's Services caseworkers. In Butler County, where Marcus' court case initiated, it is not uncommon for GALs to serve more than one hundred children at a time. They are required to visit children at least once every three months. Three months is a long time in the life of a young child. After all, Marcus lived with David and Liz Carroll for three months. A lot can happen to a child in three months. A lot did happen.

The juvenile court magistrate approved every service provided to Marcus and every aspect of his care. Marcus received foster care services, developmental assessments, and at least one psychiatric consultation during which he was prescribed medication (Lifeway for Youth Response to Marcus Fiesel Case). He also underwent diagnostic testing through Cincinnati Children's

Hospital Medical Center. The court approved any visitation he had with his mother and siblings and decided whether visits were supervised or unsupervised by a caseworker.

Although the magistrate holds a tremendous amount of power in making decisions regarding foster children, these decisions are only as good as the information provided to him or her, and the court's involvement does not end once the magistrate decides a child should be placed in foster care. A magistrate continues monitoring the case for months, sometimes years. For the duration of a case, a magistrate will make dozens of decisions regarding placement, services, and visitation for foster children based on information he or she receives from the adults in the courtroom.

In Hamilton County Juvenile Court, a child's case is reviewed every three to six months. During these review hearings, the magistrate collects information from all legal parties about the family's progress toward reunification and how the child is doing. If a Butler County magistrate heard a review of Marcus' case at some point following his placement with the Carrolls, he or she would have likely been told how well Marcus was doing. He was receiving the necessary medical testing and services to address his developmental delays. He was stable in the Carrolls' home and they were willing to keep him long term if necessary. The magistrate could have easily taken this information and concluded that Marcus' best interests were being met. The caseworkers in and out of the Carrolls' home never suspected he was being abused or neglected. How could the magistrate believe differently?

Each system-related professional had a job to do on Marcus' behalf. The majority of duties lies with the Children's Services caseworker. This person requested a licensed foster home for Marcus and placed him there. He or she would have been required to have monthly face-to-face contact with Marcus. The Children's Services caseworker also arranged services for Marcus such as a specialist to help him prevail over his developmental delays as well as other medical and psychological testing. If Donna were actively working toward reunification, the Children's Services caseworker would have arranged all services for her and monitored her compliance and progress. He or she also would have been responsible for arranging weekly family visitation so Marcus could visit with Donna and his siblings.

Marcus' Lifeway caseworker was responsible for conducting weekly foster home visits, ensuring Marcus got to medical and other appointments and supporting the Carrolls in their role.

Marcus' GAL was required to visit Marcus in his foster home less regularly and to investigate all aspects of his case. She would also have evaluated Donna's ability to care for him and investigate whether she completed court-ordered services. She would then use this information to make recommendations to the judge about what was in Marcus' best interest.

Marcus' Children's Services caseworker and his GAL were legal parties to his court case. An attorney represented his caseworker, and his GAL was an attorney. An attorney also represented Donna. If these people could not agree on issues related to Marcus, trial would occur. Balancing parental rights against Marcus' best interests, a magistrate would make decisions about his future.

When caseworkers have too many children to monitor, they cannot effectively manage their caseloads. For caseworkers to do their job with some success, it is critical that they manage only a small number of families. The Child Welfare League of America recommends caseloads of between twelve and fifteen children per worker. Across the nation, the average caseload for a child welfare worker is between twenty-four and thirty-one children (National Association of Social Work, 2004). Because this number is simply a recommendation, it is not enforceable by law. How often do caseloads fall within the suggested range? Not very often.

As a former Children's Services caseworker, I managed a case involving a mother named Denise and her eight children who had been placed in five different homes scattered throughout the city. The passing of the file included a 20-minute conversation with the previous caseworker who had resigned her position, as had the last three caseworkers the family had worked with over the past year. What I learned was that Denise often left the children home alone, sometimes for two or three days. There was never any food in the house, and sometimes, unidentified men were found scattered throughout the apartment, much like empty beer bottles and cigarette cartons. Four different men fathered the eight children. Two were in prison and the mother could not remember the identity of the other two. The family's case file had seven volumes, and I never really had time to sit down and read it thoroughly. I was always too busy attending to the crisis at hand.

The oldest child, Kim, was fourteen, and flat out angry. She was two grade levels behind in school, likely because her mother never sent her and relied on her to help with the younger children. Kim never smiled and never engaged in conversation with me when I visited. She stabbed people with pencils at school more times than I could count, and was constantly in trouble. She had changed foster homes a half dozen times in the previous year, and was living at a group home for troubled girls.

Her next youngest brother, Kewaun, age twelve, kept his problems and his anger to himself, which meant he never really got a lot of notice from me. Kenny came next at ten. He lived in the same foster home with Kewaun, and functioned at the level of a five-year-old due to a head trauma he suffered as a toddler after falling down a flight of stairs. Kenny had special education services at school and physical and occupational therapy each week. Their foster parents refused to take Kenny to all of his appointments, which left it to me to figure out how he would get where he needed to be each week. Additionally, his foster parents would not attend any school meetings for him.

Justice, age eight, and Gentry, age seven, lived with very nice foster parents who responded to the school every time they were called and told that Justice was fighting with other students. Both Justice and Gentry were one grade behind. They were tall and large for their age, and making friends with others did not come easily to either of them.

Jerome was six and had the most serious behavior problems of all the children. He had scars on his arms from a butcher knife he used to stab the roaches that roamed his mother's apartment. He cussed every adult he laid eyes on, and never held back a little fist when he didn't get his way. He had never been in preschool or kindergarten, and when I drove him to school for his first day, the principal refused to let me leave him there. Jerome had entered the building in a frenzy, running down the halls screaming and tearing pictures off the walls. Not having any idea what to do, I drove him back to his foster home. On the way, he attempted to jump out of the car. Thank God, I had the child locks employed.

He blew out of three foster homes before we found a foster mother who was strong and gentle enough to manage him. Soon after he was placed with her, she and I met with the principal. I was impressed with how successfully she had argued for Jerome to return to a classroom and agreed to accompany him each day until he was able to acclimate to the environment.

Martin, age three, was born profoundly deaf, and his mother had failed to get any medical treatment or help for him. Like his big bother, Jerome, he didn't follow car rules either, and as quickly as Houdini, he always managed to slip out of his car seat. Any attempts to verbally redirect him from the front failed because of his hearing loss. When it was time for him to be transported to family visits or medical appointments, two adults had to ride in the car with him. One day I went to visit him in his foster home, and his foster mother was beside herself. He had gone to the bathroom and smeared his feces all over the wall and the shower curtain. This kind of behavior is not uncommon among children who are experiencing tremendous anger with no way to communicate.

The youngest child, Edwaun, age eighteen months also lived with Martin. The first time I met him was during a weekly family visit with his mom and siblings. He tottled around, carrying a bottle full of Mountain Dew. He walked around aimlessly, occasionally using the bottle to whack a sibling on the head. My jaw dropped when the "F" word spewed out of his mouth.

As you can imagine, monitoring Kim's group home and all four foster homes, ensuring that each of the children received all the services they needed, including educational and counseling services, and then arranging for and verifying the mother's compliance with court ordered services was a monumental task. Coordinating weekly family visits was nothing short of a three-ring circus, involving two co-workers and myself. It took three people just to pick up the children and bring them to a central meeting place where they could see each other and their mother.

I could have easily spent forty hours per week working with only this family, and it still would not have been enough. I noticed that Kim loved to sing. I overheard her once singing with such depth and feeling I stopped dead in my tracks. She was singing her pain, and it was beautiful. Maybe voice lessons, or participation in a choir, could be her sanctuary at a critical and painful time in her life. That idea came and went quickly as I was trying to arrange Kenny's medical appointments, therapy for Jerome, and appointments with specialists for Martin's hearing loss. When doctors were discussing treatment options for Martin, including cochlear implants, I left the decisions up to Denise and the administrators at my agency. I didn't have the time to fully research all the options. Although singing may have been a powerful, positive thing in Kim's life, the time and money it would take to arrange the extras simply did not exist. This was just one family on my caseload of twenty-five. Although I did the very best job I could, it was never enough. As part of my job, I reported to the court about the care of each of the children and the issues they faced. Was I accurate and up to date? To the best of my knowledge, I was. Is it possible I missed things while monitoring their care? I certainly may have. Back then, any concerns I may have had about missing something were brushed aside as soon as the phone rang and there was a new problem to solve.

After spending two years on the front lines of child abuse and neglect, I just couldn't continue. The work was demanding and heart breaking. Newly married and expecting a baby, I realized that the trauma of the job and the late nights wouldn't be conducive to my life as a young mother. At the end of my two-year tenure, I was a veteran. Many other co-workers came and went during that timeframe. Nationally, the average turnover rate in the child welfare workforce is about 35% (U.S. General Accounting Office, 2003). When children are placed in foster care, they lose everything familiar to them. Many times, they lose their siblings, their school, their friends, and even their clothes or favorite stuffed animals. They will likely lose their caseworker, the one face they have come to recognize, within months.

Caseworkers are not the only professionals working with these children who struggle with the problem of having too much to do in too little time. The GAL has the critical responsibility of independently monitoring a child's placement and services. However, this person serves on court-involved cases, meaning that a majority of their daily calendar is eaten up by trials and other court hearings. If a GAL spends six hours per day in court, there is not much time left for home visits and team meetings.

Mental health therapists also play a critical role in helping young foster children overcome trauma and begin to heal. This therapy can only work if the other professionals involved with the child have the opportunity to talk to the therapist about a child's progress and implement their recommendations. Foster children are generally covered by government-subsidized health insurance, or Medicaid, and therapists are only permitted to bill one hour per week per child. My experience has been that some therapists will refuse to talk with GALs or attend team meetings, saying that they are not paid to participate in such activities and therefore are unwilling to do so. This greatly reduces the ability of a child's therapy to be successful and diminishes the ability of the GAL and social worker to make informed recommendations to the court.

When professionals come and go throughout the life of a case, details of children's lives get lost in the shuffle. Children in foster care routinely change foster home placements, caseworkers, therapists, and physicians. These are the fingers through which children like Marcus slip. The potential also exists for important information to never make its way into a courtroom.

Children who are raised in the foster care system ultimately pay the price for this lack of continuity and information sharing. They suffer visibly when important information fails to get to the right people. Their invisible scars run just as deep and are just as painful.

One of my cases as a Children's Services caseworker involved seven-year-old Mandy. Her mother, Rachel, had been in and out of drug rehab. Her random urine screens were always clean and she denied any ongoing substance abuse. Even so, she could never manage to get Mandy to school, resulting in an allegation of educational neglect. One of my unannounced home visits found Mandy and Rachel playing Monopoly, and when I asked why she wasn't in school, Rachel replied that Mandy didn't have the required uniform. I reminded her that the social worker from the school would provide it; she just needed to get her there.

One day when I stopped in to check on the family, no one was home. I didn't think much of it, and returned to my office. Later in the day, I received a message that Mandy and Rachel were at the hospital. Mandy was being treated for third degree burns to her arm. Rachel had left her home alone while she went to a neighbor's house. Mandy was burned while attempting to fix a lunch of fried eggs. Rachel was neglectful in her supervision of Mandy, and as a result, Mandy went to live with relatives.

Ten years later, I exited an elevator at juvenile court and was greeted by a teenager. She called me by name and waved excitedly. I smiled and waved back, and as I checked in, the security guard told me her name. It was Mandy. I spent time catching up with her, and she filled me in on the details of her life. She grew quiet and held up her arm. "Do you know how I got these scars? I can't remember, and no one else remembers either."

"I remember what happened to your arm. It happened during the winter of 1994, a few weeks after Christmas. Your mom had left you home alone and you were hungry. You found some eggs in the refrigerator and decided to fry them. The skillet was heavy and your little hands weren't strong enough to hold it while you were trying to flip them. The skillet landed on your arm and big blisters grew. When your mom came home and found you crying, she took you to the Shriner's Burn Institute near Children's Hospital. You had to stay there for a few days while the doctor's treated your arm. When it was time for you to leave the hospital, you went to live with your Aunt Linda because your mom couldn't take care of you and keep you safe."

"I remember only a little about living with Aunt Linda," Mandy confided. "She drank a lot and a social worker came and took me away from her. But you weren't my caseworker then." We sat together for about ten minutes until my case was called. She told me that she had lived in many different places and was now in an apartment on her own and getting help from caseworkers who were teaching her how to live independently. She never went to live with Rachel again, who had relapsed on drugs. Her eyes searched mine for answers to the questions she held closest to her heart, and when we parted, I could see the wheels turning in her mind as she made sense of the history I had given back to her.

How could she not know how she had been scarred? Still court involved ten years later, she had run through dozens of county caseworkers. She had also bounced from relative to relative, each placement failing. With each change in caseworker and each change in caregiver, pieces of her life were lost. Who can be the holder of these critical tidbits while children make their way through childhood? When children are unable to make sense of their past and their history, they are less likely to make good, grounded decisions about their futures.

When the facts about Marcus' death were revealed, people involved in his care looked at each other and pointed fingers. How could certified foster parents, two grown adults, pin his arms behind him, wrap him in a blanket, bind him in packing tape, lay him in a playpen, and shut the door? How could this happen? Something went terribly wrong. Whose fault was it? Lifeway for Youth blamed the foster parents. Children's Services blamed Lifeway for Youth. Some blamed Marcus' mother for letting him go. Marcus' GAL and the court were silent.

While blaming the professionals may make us feel better, the real discussion to be had involves looking at the structure of the system and how it functions. After all, not many people are vying for the job of working in the system. It's not an easy job, and to do it well requires a lot of skill, and a tremendous amount of support. It is a job with significant responsibility.

And, it's painful. It's devastating to see helpless children abused and neglected by their parents.

As a GAL, my days are spent conducting home visits with infants and toddlers who have been beaten, starved, raped, or born drug-addicted. I also spend a significant amount of time advocating for them in court. When my workday is over, I return to the haven of my own home, robust with the noise and activity of my own three children. I sit on sidelines at ball fields and watch parents chase their giggling toddlers and play with their preschoolers while their older children practice. The two worlds are so vastly different. They operate side by side yet never seem to touch each other. However, the answers to the horrors facing some of these children's little lives exist only in the community of families around them.

A half million children like Marcus are drifting through foster care, dependent on a system that too often fails to meet their needs. Blaming the current system will not fix it, and looking the other way is no longer an option.

As long as there are children, there will be children who cannot depend on their parents to take care of them. As long as the government shoulders responsibility for their daily care, there will be children who suffer. Until the community steps forward to right the wrongs of vulnerable kids, their childhoods will vanish, along with our hope for a better future for all of our children.

CHAPTER 3

Baby Steps

"FAITH IS CATCHING UP quite nicely now. When she first came here, she didn't move from her waist down."

Faith's foster mother was filling me in on the young girl's latest achievements. At ten months old, she was finally beginning to bear some weight on her legs. She no longer cried when her foster mother put her on the floor to encourage her to scoot around and explore. She couldn't crawl yet, but she was getting there. The first time she discovered that she could kick her legs, she was amazed and surprised. Her shock gave way to interest, and she kicked again as if the first time didn't really happen. Then she kicked again and again, her face lighting up with pride. The day Faith kicked her legs and discovered they could move was cause for celebration.

Faith wasn't paralyzed in some freak accident. Her parents weren't told she would never walk. She didn't defy outrageous medical odds, unless you count the odds stacked against her as a neglected infant. Faith's home for the first seven months of her life had been a baby swing. With the exception of propped bottles and the occasional diaper change, she was pretty much left alone.

Faith was eight months old when I first met her, although the mop of jet-black hair was so long and thick it seemed like it should have belonged to a much older baby. It fell softly around her dark complexion and big, dark eyes. She struck me as the most serious baby I had ever seen. When I caught sight of her precious little face, I thought how funny it is that we still believe babies don't really know what's going on. It was clear that Faith knew exactly what was happening around her, and she was going to take it all in before making any decisions about how she felt about it.

Two months later, it seemed like Faith had made her decision. It was all going to be OK. She smiled easily and squealed happily, as she crawled around the carpeted floor of her foster home, reaching for books and toys and occasionally the family dog.

Faith, like Marcus Fiesel, was born into this world facing significant obstacles. Faith was born to a single, nineteen-year-old mom who was not prepared for the challenges of raising a baby on her own. Maria sported the same jet-black hair and dark eyes as her baby. She was a little thing, no more than five feet tall and weighing well under a hundred pounds, and the task of raising a baby on her own was gigantic.

Unable to cope with the tasks Faith required of her, Maria simply put Faith in a baby swing, propped a bottle for her, and walked away. All Maria managed to give Faith was an occasional diaper change and formula. Faith likely cried out, as all newborns do, when she was hungry or wet. But when no one came, Faith realized her efforts were futile and she gave up trying to get her needs met. She adapted to her life in the baby swing. Tragically, she wasn't growing or developing, as she should have been.

As a child, Maria had been sexually abused for years by an uncle, and so had severed ties with her family. She had no support system to call upon, and suffered from severe depression. She had no job, no income, and no idea who Faith's father was. When the landlord served her with an eviction notice, the apartment was filthy. Soiled diapers and moldy bottles littered the floor. Old food overflowed in the kitchen. Maria was sleeping so soundly she could hardly be awakened. She was oblivious to Faith, who was asleep in her baby swing, the battery long dead. Maria was hospitalized for psychiatric treatment and Faith was placed in foster care.

Faith and Marcus Fiesel shared the same potential for growth and development that all babies share. Despite the vast differences in the families and the circumstances that children are born into, most babies are programmed to develop in the same way at essentially the same rate, barring any medical or social problems.

Maria had sporadic prenatal care. Faith was born full-term and was healthy when she was discharged from the hospital. She was set to follow a predictable pattern of development. She would hold her head up before she learned to sit up. She would develop bigger muscles before smaller ones. She would gain control in her arms before she would master the ability to purposefully move her little fingers. She would crawl before she would stand, and stand before she would walk. Even though Faith was set to learn and grow, her chances of doing so were diminished by neglect. Spending most of her early life in a baby swing meant that her legs weren't moving, and muscles weren't developing. Without an adult to talk to her and encourage her, she wasn't motivated to make noise. "Significant parental mental health problems (particularly maternal depression), substance abuse, and family violence impose heavy developmental burdens on young children" (Zero to Three, 2001).

Babies have a lot of work to do in the first year of life. They work hard at learning what we often consider the little things. They struggle to hold their heads up beginning around the age of one month. They master that, and then begin attempting to push their bodies up using their arms. At the same time, they begin to try rolling over. They wiggle from side to side, day in and day out. Then one day, after so much practice, they flip from back to belly and grin from ear to ear at this newfound trick they have just mastered. They begin to scoot around and soon they learn to master the crawling position. They get on all fours and try to crawl. They rock back and forth, back and forth without ever getting anywhere. And then, one day, it happens. All the movements come together and off they go, crawling slowly at first, as if they can't believe they are moving in this fashion. Within days, they are crawling pros, moving at the speed of light, rounding corners and dissolving into fits of giggles when their parents chase after them.

Child development occurs in steps. Imagine looking up a flight of stairs, each step representing a baby's developmental milestone. The steps ascend in the same fashion for most babies, barring medical problems. As long as babies steadily make their way up the stairs, they are in good shape. Some babies take longer to get up the steps and that's OK, as long as they keep moving. Other baby's whiz up the steps at record pace, and that's OK too. But if he or she stays stuck on one step too long, or moves a step or two back, there is potentially a problem. When caregivers change and caseworkers change, such as in the lives of foster children, these problems can be missed. No one in this scenario knows how long a baby has been on a step, or whether the baby has descended a step or two.

When infants are abused or neglected, their progress towards meeting developmental milestones is interrupted. Their little bodies fail to develop. They may appear to be of average size and stature for their age, but they are not growing in critical ways. These babies aren't exploring the world around them, or how their bodies move and belong in this world. A baby can't learn how to hold his head up if he is left lying in a crib all day. He won't reach to grab a toy without encouragement. If an angry adult physically abuses him because he won't quit crying, his little body will experience a significant amount of stress. "Infants and toddlers are extremely vulnerable to the effects of maltreatment. Its impact on emotional, developmental and physical health can have life-long implications if not properly addressed" (Cohen, Julie and Youcha, 2004, p. 15). A baby relies on adults around him or her to provide support and an environment conducive to his growth. Without this, babies, along with their muscles, wither.

Have you ever planted a garden? You carefully prepare the soil and plant the seeds several inches apart. It takes time and effort to plant the seeds, ensure they get the right amount of exposure to sunlight and frequent watering. Looking at your infant garden all you really see is dirt. One day you notice that tiny green shoots are emerging from the ground. You continue attending to them carefully, and the shoots grow bigger and stronger. The day arrives when they form tiny buds. You are thrilled at the sight of the new life growing. Your efforts continue, and the buds open to beautifully colored flowers. As the flowers grow in strength and numbers, you realize you cannot even see the soil beneath them, for all that is visible is green foliage and vibrant flowers.

Babies' brains are somewhat the same. The seeds of a baby's brain are called neurons. At birth, a baby's brain contains nearly one hundred billion neurons (Nash, 1997). These are like the planted seeds, ready to grow with tender care. The care the neurons experience will determine how they grow and come together. "Brain development consists of an ongoing process of wiring and re-wiring the connections among the neurons" (Hawley, 2000). If babies are nurtured and supported, the neurons will connect and strengthen, allowing the brain to grow. "Infants and children who are rarely spoken to, who are exposed to few toys, and who have little opportunity to explore and experiment with their environment may fail to fully develop the neural connections and pathways that facilitate later learning" (Hawley, 2000). If the brain is not handled with tender care, if it is left lying in a crib or in a baby swing with little interaction, the neurons, or seeds, won't grow. Faith was shutting down after her many months in the baby swing. Just as her arms, legs, and torso weren't gaining strength and coordinated movement, her cognitive and social abilities weren't developing either. Children like Faith will likely struggle academically and socially. "Despite their normal genetic endowment, these children are at a significant intellectual disadvantage, and are likely to require costly special education or other remedial services when they enter school" (Hawley, 2000).

If Faith had remained in a baby swing, without an adult actively engaging her, she may have grown physically, but her ability to successfully navigate her surroundings in the future wouldn't be so good. Faith may have experienced chronic speech delays, balance problems, and poor coordination. She may have had trouble understanding how her body moves and works, and be overwhelmed with adjusting to a childhood classroom with other more confident, coordinated children.

Each spring, I look forward to signs of new life in nature around me. I watch the trees near my home very closely, waiting for the day when it looks as if Mother Nature took a paintbrush and gingerly coated each brown branch with light green hues. I can't resist the garden centers, whose grounds boast beautiful shades of red, yellow, and purple flowers. I eagerly snatch them up, come home and put them in the ground. I water them and wait for them to grow. Many times, I end up disappointed, because I didn't take the time to prepare the soil for their arrival. Despite the watering and the very best organic fertilizer, sometimes my flowers just don't grow.

Like flowers that thrive in carefully cultivated soil, a baby's attachment to his or her caregiver is rooted in loving-kindness, in a relationship that offers nurturance, comfort, consistency, and routine. A thriving, growing baby depends on this kind of relationship as much as he or she depends on food and water.

Brain research has exploded in the last two decades. We now have scientific evidence to support what child development professionals suspected all along; nurtured babies, who have a consistent caregiver providing safety and routine, flourish as they grow. Beyond the basic needs of food, clothing, and shelter, these babies' brains rely on protection, stability, and nurturing for their full development. The degree to which early life experiences shape the brain is astounding. "It is estimated that 85% of a baby's brain growth occurs in the first three years of life" (Bruner, Goldbert, & Kot, 1999). Abuse and neglect significantly hamper the brain's ability to grow. Consider that approximately 39,000 infants are placed in foster care (U.S. Department of Health and Human Services, AFCARS report, 2001). Twenty-one percent of all children in foster care were admitted prior to their first birthday (Wulczyn & Hislop, 2002). Many of these children have missed out on a chance to live in environments that encourage their growth and development.

Faith was lucky in the sense that the adults responsible for her while in foster care made sure she received early intervention services to address her developmental delays. Faith's evaluation revealed delays in gross and fine motor skills, meaning her big muscles and little muscles were not developing. She was also speech delayed. She was not babbling or making any verbal sounds at the time of her foster care placement. Speech and physical therapists worked with Faith to ensure progress in these areas.

While early intervention services played a crucial role in helping Faith make gains in her physical development, these gains would not have been possible if she did not have a healthy and loving relationship with an adult who would meet her needs consistently. All growth and development is rooted in attachment. Without it, infants and toddlers lose out on a chance to explore and learn about the world with a sense of wonder. Even if Faith was assisted by physical therapists, speech therapists, and occupational therapists, but lacked a nurturing home with a loving caregiver who was attentive to her needs, her progress would have been questionable.

Faith's newly formed attachment with her foster parents made the gains in her growth possible. Faith's foster mother got down on the floor with her and encouraged Faith to move toward her. With a pleasant voice and lots of encouragement, the foster mother reached her arms out to Faith and called for her. This type of movement didn't come easy for Faith at first, but her desire to be in her foster mother's loving arms provided the motivation she needed to work hard at moving her body. Without that motivation, without the desire to be showered with kisses upon her arrival, Faith may or may not have moved. Her attachment to her foster mother is what brought it all together.

Marcus Fiesel also received similar evaluations and interventions. Early intervention screenings exist to determine whether an infant or toddler is experiencing developmental delays. They are available to all children free of charge, regardless of a family's income. Infants and toddlers in foster care are automatically eligible for complete diagnostic assessments regarding every area of development. Because they have been abused or neglected, they get to skip the initial screening and go directly to full-blown evaluations.

Prior to Marcus' death, an early intervention specialist was involved in the decision to place him with Liz and David Carroll. He was evaluated at Cincinnati Children's Hospital and had been scheduled for an MRI. Varying reports suggested he was autistic. His Lifeway caseworker testified at Liz Carroll's murder trial that Marcus' mental age was half his chronological age, meaning he functioned at the level of an eighteen-month-old. It appeared that services were in place to help Marcus improve his development and functioning, but the bulk of his care was in the hands of his foster parents. They would be responsible for working with him every day to help him make gains in his growth and functioning.

Even if Marcus had the very best specialists working with him every day to help him overcome his delays, his progress would have been hampered by his lack of attachment with adults who loved him and could take care of him. Let's imagine Marcus did not receive any professional help, but enjoyed emotionally healthy and nurturing relationships with his caregivers. In this scenario, he would have had a better chance for success. Healthy attachments to caregivers are more important than interventions offered by skilled professionals. These attachments pave the way for interventions to be successful.

Federal and state laws recommend that all foster care children be referred for early intervention services. Children's Services caseworkers should refer children under the age of three for these services under the Early and Periodic Screening, Diagnosis, and Treatment Provisions of Federal Medicaid Law (Federal Medicaid Law, 2000). The goal of this federal law is to ensure vulnerable children are receiving interventions, if necessary. This hasn't exactly worked out the way the government planned.

A staggering 50% or more of foster children have untreated developmental delays including motor development problems, hearing and vision problems, growth retardation, and speech-language delays (Dicker and Gordon, 2002). This contributes to setting the stage for challenges later in life, particularly when they enter school and are significantly behind their counterparts.

While there are federal laws to ensure that foster children have access to developmental assessments and services, no laws currently exist to ensure foster children have access to a healthy attachment with an adult. Without attachment, the best developmental services by the most skilled therapists are compromised.

Faith's delays were obvious, as were Marcus Fiesel's. At seven months, Faith could not hold her head up, make eye contact, or smile spontaneously. At age three, Marcus could not communicate verbally or follow simple commands. For many foster children, developmental delays are not so obvious. A caseworker may easily overlook the quiet toddler who doesn't talk, particularly if the foster parent does not report the child's silence as a concern. Some delays are only seen over a period of time. If the same adults or professionals aren't watching this development over time, young children are more likely to have their delays go undetected and untreated.

Pediatricians are often a good line of defense in detecting developmental delays. Well-baby checks are frequent in the first year of life. Babies are monitored at birth, one to two weeks, one month, two months, four months, six month, nine months, and twelve months in attempts to identify any medical problems. These checkups are also designed to monitor how the baby is doing on the staircase of her development. The pediatrician is able to look at the baby's development over time and see a problem, however slight, and can work with the parent to remedy it.

But babies in foster care often don't benefit from a single doctor who has monitored them since their birth, nor a consistent caregiver providing information to medical professionals. When babies are placed in foster care their medical records don't automatically follow them, if there are any records to begin with.

When Faith was placed in foster care at age seven months, her foster mother took her to the doctor. Faith's biological mother was in a psychiatric hospital and unavailable to attend the appointment with her. Faith's caseworker delegated the responsibility of maintaining medical care to the foster parents; therefore, the caseworker did not attend. The foster mother didn't know Faith's birth weight or whether she had received any immunizations prior to coming into foster care. She didn't know at what age Faith held a rattle or followed the voice of a caregiver. She didn't know whether there was any medical history of importance. Under these circumstances pediatricians do the best they can, but it is largely a guessing game when there are few clues provided in determining an infant's growth and development early in life.

Though only Faith's foster mother and pediatrician attended her appointment, her medical care remained in the hands of many people. Her medical history was in the hands of her biological mother. Faith's legal custodian, the Children's Services caseworker, was the only person able to consent to medical treatment. Faith's foster mother was the only person who could articulate how Faith was progressing day to day. Many people held separate and critical pieces of the puzzle of Faith's medical history and development. This is true for many foster children.

Consider the case of Todd. His mother and her boyfriend called 911 when she was in labor. An ambulance responded to their apartment and found drug paraphernalia littering the kitchen table. Todd's mom and her boyfriend were both transported to the hospital, though the boyfriend jumped out of the ambulance when it was stopped at a traffic light. He told the mother he would catch up with her later, after he got a case of beer from a gas station on the corner. Todd's mom went to the hospital. He was born addicted to cocaine with traces of cocaine and marijuana in his system. She had no prenatal care and left the hospital immediately after he was born, without Todd. She had no plans to take care of him and barely stuck around long enough to lay eyes on her baby.

Todd was placed with a foster family when he was discharged from the hospital. A routine medical appointment detected unusually large head growth for his age when he was six months old. His pediatrician referred him for an MRI to rule out any neurological problems. His foster parents took Todd for the MRI. They assumed the caseworker would contact them if they needed to take Todd to any additional appointments. The caseworker assumed that if any follow up was needed the doctor would call the foster parents to notify them. Meanwhile, the test results indicated a need for further testing at a neurology clinic. These results and recommendations were sent to the caseworker and immediately buried in a case file.

Two months later, I became Todd's GAL. He was eight months old. I came across the MRI results in a copy of his case file. Not knowing how to read them or what they meant, I called the clinic to get clarification on his medical care and any needs he might have. I learned that their attempts to reach both the caseworker and the foster parents were unsuccessful, and Todd was due back immediately for further testing. His medical care nearly slipped through the hands of the people entrusted to ensure his needs were met.

In efforts to ensure that they receive necessary medical care, the vast majority of foster children receive a medical card upon placement. This card is a government-subsidized health insurance policy and is available to children whose parents cannot otherwise afford it. It's a good thing they receive medical coverage, because 80% of foster children have at least one chronic health condition and 25% have three or more chronic problems—three to seven times the rate found among other children living in poverty (Dicker and Gordon, 2002). Medical care is within the reach of every foster child. Unfortunately, a medical card does not guarantee that foster children will receive even routine medical care.

While foster children suffering from untreated developmental delays and lacking routine medical care face tremendous obstacles, young children who are exposed to family violence experience even greater challenges.

Adam and Sarah lived with their parents until the ages of four and two, respectively. During these years, exposure to domestic violence was a regular occurrence for them. On three separate occasions a Children's Services caseworker investigated the family following allegations of domestic violence. A neighbor called Children's Services to report she had overheard the parents fighting one night, and the next morning observed the mother with a black eye. Another time, a family friend called Children's Services to report that there were many people in and out of the home and that fighting and screaming were a common occurrence. Each time, the case was investigated and closed, due to lack of evidence to support the caller's claims.

The violence continued and escalated. One day, Adam and Sarah's mother, Jessica, invited an acquaintance into their home. The children were present when Jessica and their father, Keith, robbed and beat him. Adam and Sarah were placed in foster care when their parents were charged and incarcerated. They did not have any relatives or family friends to take them in.

Adam and Sarah arrived at their foster home at 11 p.m. with just the clothes on their backs. They were starving, filthy, and lice-infested. Adam's foster mother undressed him for his bath and found bruises on his back. A closer look at Sarah revealed bruises and scratches behind her earlobes. After a late meal and baths, Adam and Sarah were laid in the first beds they had ever seen.

Adam pointed to the bed and looked afraid of it. He had no idea what it was.

His foster mother was shocked, but tried to hide her surprise. "This is a bed," she explained to Adam. "This is where people sleep at night time. It is very soft and the blanket will keep you warm. Haven't you ever seen a bed before?" she asked gently.

"No," Adam said simply, and eyed the bed suspiciously.

"Where did you sleep when you lived with your mom and dad?" Adam shrugged his shoulders. Wherever he slept, it was clear it was not in a bed.

They didn't sleep much that first night. Both Adam and Sarah screamed, cried, and kicked the walls. They refused to be consoled by their foster parents. They became hysterical at the foster parents' attempts to comfort them. Adam tore the sheets off his bed and pulled drawers from the dresser. Sarah alternated between screaming and sitting quietly, her gaze fixed. It was a long night in their new home. After several hours, both of the children fell into an exhausted sleep.

Within days, it became apparent that the children had suffered extreme neglect and abuse while living with their parents. They did not want to be touched by anyone. Adam lashed out in rage any time his foster parents laid a hand on him. Sarah's response was less violent. She retreated into a world where she could not be reached. One day Sarah tripped over a book lying on the floor and bumped her head on a table. Rather than allow her foster mother to comfort her, she wrapped her arms around herself and hummed.

Both Adam and Sarah hoarded food, worried that regular meals would not occur. Every night at dinner, Adam would stuff food into his pockets; dinner rolls, corn, even hamburgers. Sarah stuffed food into her little mouth so fast that she gagged herself at least once each meal. Dinnertime became a power struggle. The foster parents tried to assure the children that they would not go hungry, but Adam and Sarah could not be convinced.

It was immediately clear that both children were developmentally delayed. Adam's speech was unintelligible and Sarah didn't speak at all. Neither child seemed to have ever experienced playing with a toy, as they had no idea what to do with a ball. Adam and Sarah could not do simple things much younger children can do. They could not scribble with crayons or hold a pencil. They were unable to stack blocks despite being shown how to do so. Adam preferred to throw the blocks as hard as he could rather than sit patiently and learn how to play.

Most troubling, however, was Adam's violent behavior toward everyone around him, particularly his sister. He was unable to handle minor stresses, such as the end of his favorite television show. As soon as it was over, Adam screamed and hit the television. He was very impulsive and his first response to any frustration was to be enraged. He would kick, scream, and set out to destroy anything in his path. When he and Sarah both wanted the same toy, Adam's response was to choke her. When his foster parents put him in time out and tried to discipline him, he responded by kicking and throwing things. When they removed everything from his reach, he turned his anger on himself, beating his head with his fists or pulling his hair. His temper tantrums would last for hours.

Chronic exposure to violence in his formative years had a toxic effect on Adam. These included physical, behavioral, and emotional effects. "Very young children who witness either domestic violence or community violence show increased irritability, immature behavior, developmental regression and increased fears" (Osofsky & Fenichel, 1994). The more prolonged the exposure to violence, the more devastating the consequences for young children. When babies are exposed to violence, their brains secrete a stress hormone called cortisol. This hormone is secreted when a person is under stress, triggering what is known as the fight or flight response. As adults, when we are faced with a perceived danger, our physiological response is automatic. Outside of our conscious awareness, we mentally assess the danger and our response to it. Babies do the same thing, though they are not able to fight or leave. This creates devastating consequences for their growing brain, including an impact on a child's IQ. "Children age five who were exposed to high levels of domestic violence have IQs about eight points lower than unexposed children. To put this number in perspective, consider that chronic lead exposure decreases children's IQs by only three or four points" (Koenen, Moffitt, Caspi, Taylor & Purcell, 2003).

Many infants and toddlers arrive in this world ready to grow. The neurons in their brains, like the seeds in your garden, are ready and waiting to be nurtured into full growth. When they are abused and neglected, this growth is stunted. The bad news is that they often suffer developmental delays, cognitive delays, physical disabilities, and mental health issues as a result of this abuse and neglect. The good news is that these devastating consequences are completely preventable.

Compare the life-long effects of abuse and neglect on young children to the impact of disease on families, such as cancer. Although significant gains have been made in treating many forms of cancer, there is still much to be done to learn more about cancer and how to treat it. To this end, money is raised to continue research, to search for cures so that it no longer destroys families. The community often joins the search for a cure by donating to the American Cancer Society or running in 5K races to raise money.

No money needs to be raised to fund research to find a cure for the long-term effects of child abuse and neglect. We know it is preventable. While cancer patients frequently have family and friends surrounding them and advocating for a cure, abused and neglected toddlers lack this supportive community.

When children suffer abuse or neglect and are removed from their families, their treatment occurs in a system that frequently exacerbates the problems from which children suffer. Hidden within the foster care system, these children are invisible to the community around them.

Not only are the effects of child abuse and neglect preventable, they are also largely treatable. With proper care, support, and assistance, young children who have been abused and neglected can recover from early traumatic experiences. Faith blossomed under the care of her foster parents. Once she began to soak up their love and attention and had a place to safely explore the world while moving around on her two chubby, little legs, she flourished. Unfortunately, the foster care system as it is currently designed cannot ensure this kind of care and support.

Children like Adam and Sarah come into foster care every day. Adam and Sarah's caseworker took nearly a month to complete the necessary paperwork to refer the children for therapy. Once the referral was made, the soonest intake appointment was not available for another month. Two months passed without any therapeutic interventions for Adam and Sarah, who had both endured horrendous trauma.

In these three months, the foster parents became increasingly stressed about their ability to handle the children. The children required vigilant supervision, as one never knew when Adam would explode into a rage. The foster parents became isolated from their own extended families. The children's behavior made it impossible for the foster family to enjoy outings with their in-laws, nieces, and nephews.

Adam and Sarah's foster parents had made many phone calls to the caseworker requesting assistance in managing the children. The foster parents felt they were in over their heads and simply had no idea how to deal with Adam's increasing violence. They were also parents to two boys, ages eight and five. Adam had a hard time adjusting to living in a home with other children. On one occasion, Adam got angry and shattered a window with a plastic baseball bat. On another, he took a pet goldfish and flushed it down the toilet. His foster siblings were devastated. While Sarah didn't exhibit the same behaviors as her brother, she was also hard to manage. She cried often, without provocation, and was difficult to soothe. She didn't like to be held. She was ridiculously independent for her age and had a tantrum when the foster mother attempted to help her with small tasks, such as pouring her milk.

Abused children may never give their foster parents that momentary reward for all the patience and selfless devotion it takes to raise them. Unfortunately, Adam and Sarah's foster parents didn't have those moments. Despite their caring, consistency, and stability, Adam and Sarah didn't seem to be responding. Adam, in particular, seemed to get more and more difficult to manage.

The caseworker offered to follow up on a previous referral made for therapy. But it was too little, too late. The foster parents were done. Three months had passed when Adam and Sarah's foster parents decided they could not continue living with the daily chaos that Adam and Sarah had brought with them.

The foster parents believed they could keep Sarah, but not Adam. He was just too much for them. They felt it was best for him to be moved to another foster home. In the interest of keeping siblings together, Sarah's bags were packed as well and they journeyed into their second foster home, exacerbating their feelings of fear and abandonment. With no control over their past and no control over their future, they were at the mercy of the system.

CHAPTER 4

Multiple Moves

LTHOUGH ADAM AND SARAH's foster parents requested their removal, their county caseworker, Lisa, had up to thirty days to locate a new foster home for them. During this time, Lisa contacted the Foster Care Unit within Children's Services. After passing on information related to the children, their needs and behaviors, Lisa received the name of a new foster family that would be willing to take them. Barring emergencies, foster care rules require that foster parents give a month's notice. Adam and Sarah remained with a foster family who had no intention of keeping them while the caseworker obtained a new placement. Many times foster children are not prepared to move into a new home or even told they will be leaving. This was the case with Adam and Sarah.

Lisa made arrangements to move the children soon after she received the name of the new foster family. She arrived to collect Adam and Sarah. The foster parents had not explained to them that they would be leaving. They had left that to Lisa. She had no idea she would be expected to tell the children they were moving. Lisa glanced at Adam and Sarah, who were watching television quietly. She entered the family room where they sat and told them she needed to talk to them. The foster parents switched off the television, much to Adam's dismay. Although he was angry, he didn't throw a temper tantrum. Lisa began tentatively. "You've been with your foster parents for a little while now, but they can't take care of you anymore. They think it would be good for you both to live with another family."

Sarah sucked her thumb and sat motionless, her little fingers clutching the arm of a teddy bear. Adam, the spokesman for the two, asked questions in rapid-fire succession.

"Why do we have to leave? Do I still get to be with Sarah? When can I see my real mom? Will we get to eat dinner tonight?" As the questions continued, confusion and fear mounted in his eyes. Following the lead of her big brother, Sarah's lip began to quiver and, still clutching her teddy bear, she shifted her little body closer to Adam.

Lisa didn't have many answers for them and felt helpless to make them feel any better. "Yes, Adam, the two of you will live together. I know you miss your real mom, but she can't visit you right now because she did some things that weren't very nice and she is learning how to treat people better. Tonight you will eat dinner with your new foster family." While Lisa made a feeble attempt to quell their rising anxiety and answer Adam's questions, the foster parents finished gathering the children's belongings and placed them in black garbage bags. More often than not, foster children do not own luggage or duffle bags. Even when they do, such things often get lost in their transient lives. It is common practice for them to move with disposable trash bags. Like the children, when the bags aren't wanted anymore, they can be tossed out.

When it was time to leave, the foster parents hugged both Adam and Sarah and told them to be good in their new home. Adam simply returned the hugs and walked away. Sarah had a harder time. She clung to the foster mother's legs and cried. The foster mother, visibly shaken, picked her up and hugged her tight. Then, she attempted to extract herself from Sarah's fierce embrace while the caseworker pried Sarah away. The caseworker carried Sarah out the front door, and when her cries subsided, she carefully placed her in the backseat next to Adam. She buckled Sarah into a car seat and drove away.

Twenty minutes passed before Lisa and the children arrived at their new foster home. She found the home easily and pulled the car into the driveway. She took note of the tidy ranch house and the lazy, black Labrador snoozing on the front porch. She led the children to the front door and knocked, Adam standing on her left and Sarah on her right. The door opened, and their new foster mother bent down to greet them. Adam and Sarah stood as still as statues, and didn't say a word.

The caseworker introduced them and returned to her car to retrieve their bags of belongings. When she entered the house, Adam and Sarah were sitting side by side on an old, comfortably worn couch. The caseworker spent fifteen minutes talking with the new foster mother about Adam and Sarah's history and behavior. When she stood up to leave, Sarah scrambled off the couch. She raced toward Lisa and hung onto her, sobbing. The foster mother untangled Sarah from the caseworker and consoled her. Adam watched this unfold and began crying too. With the foster mother's encouragement, Lisa said good-bye to Adam and Sarah and closed the door behind her.

Like Adam and Sarah, Marcus Fiesel moved from home to home. He lived with his mother and then was placed in a foster home. He left his foster family to return to his mother. He stayed with his mother for only six months before he was taken away again due to neglect. He was again placed in foster care.

It is important to note that Marcus did not go back to his first foster home. The foster care system cannot guarantee a child will return to a previous foster home if reunification with his or her parent fails. Professionals can inquire as to whether a child can return to a previous home, but many times, it is not possible. Foster homes are licensed for a certain number of children. If the home is full, additional children may not be accepted, even if they resided there before. This prevents the return of a child to a familiar place.

When Marcus was placed in foster care for the second time, he went to live with a family he did not know. This foster family had difficulty caring for Marcus. At Liz Carroll's murder trial, his Lifeway caseworker testified that Marcus was aggressive toward the foster mother's granddaughter. He needed around the clock supervision. Caring for Marcus was a full time job, and an exhausting one at that. He was in this foster home for less than two weeks before his foster mother requested his removal. As a result of this request, Marcus was moved to the Carrolls' home on May 5, 2006. By the age of three, Marcus had lived in at least five different places.

What would your life be like if you had to move five times in the past three years, not because you wanted to, but because you had no choice? What would it be like to move in with strangers? Think back to celebrating birthdays or holidays with your family. Now think about never celebrating in the same place twice or with the same people. Think about going to bed every night, wondering where you would move next, where you would get your next meal, and who would be your family.

In contrast, think about how families and organizations work together to transition more privileged children. Many preparations are made for young children when they begin school. Preschool is a big deal in the lives of these children and parents who are sending them off into the great big world of formal education. Often, parents research preschool programs. They visit the schools and programs, talk with other parents, and after much consideration, they enroll their son or daughter.

Before a new year begins, parents receive letters detailing important information about the upcoming year. Teachers mail their students little postcards to welcome them. Schools host Meet the Teacher Night, inviting students and their families to visit the school. Have you ever been to this kind of event? There is an excitement in the air as teachers, parents, and children come together to get the lay of the land before the first day.

Children are usually hesitant at first. They look around the classroom and hide their faces against their parents' legs when they are introduced to other children. They get a chance to see where they will sit and where they will hang their coat. The big day arrives and off they go, sporting Barbie and Spiderman backpacks that are nearly as large as their little bodies.

For foster children, preparation for any significant change is often hard to come by. The foster care system is not necessarily equipped to deal proactively with issues like placement changes for children. The nature of the system often demands that caseworkers respond to the case that requires immediate attention. They triage the crises of any given day and prioritize them accordingly.

In a hospital emergency room, patients are treated according to the severity of their injuries. However, if a person suffering from the flu continually gets bumped to the bottom of the list as more critical patients are arriving, problems can arise. Assume the emergency room is at capacity and staff is barely able to triage the patients coming in. The flu victim is told to have a seat in the waiting room. Hours pass. Eventually the person becomes severely dehydrated and immediate attention is now a matter of life or death. The severe dehydration has damaged the person's organs. Treatment occurs, but now overnight hospitalization is required. It's a much longer road to recovery.

Much like busy, under-staffed hospitals, Children's Services agencies also frequently attend to children who require immediate attention. Infants and toddlers fly beneath the radar more often than older children whose behavior is demanding.

It would not be uncommon for Lisa to set Adam and Sarah aside while she attended to other children with more urgent problems. Lisa managed a caseload of seventeen other families in addition to Adam and Sarah. Arranging an opportunity for Adam and Sarah to meet and visit with new foster parents would have taken Lisa away from the other children who had more pressing issues, such as a desperate call from a suicidal teenager, or a phone message from seven-year-old Johnny's teacher who is concerned because he hasn't been in school for three days. Lisa is forced to put out fires that are raging every day. Suddenly, Adam and Sarah are looking a lot better off than some children on her other cases.

The reality is that the time and attention to thoughtful transition from one home to another is absolutely critical. This planning allows a child to understand and feel more comfortable with the change. Planning for the transition also helps a new family get to know the child. Transitioning allows a stronger foundation for good relationships to be built. When solid foundations are laid, foster families and children are better able to weather the storms that childhood trauma brings.

Traumatized young children often struggle with significant fears and vulnerabilities. Countless times over the years, I have met children whose first question is, "Are you going to take me away?" Imagine seeing a social worker and immediately assuming your life is about to be turned upside down. What would it be like to live like this?

Living with this kind of stress impacts children's behavior, increasing stress on the families who care for them. Children test boundaries. It is perfectly natural for a child who has been moved around to test the commitment of a caregiver. This fear and anxiety often turns into tantrums, testing the rules of the home, and angry outbursts that can be mitigated only by stability and routine, along with nurturing from an adult sensitive to the needs, temperament, and development of a child.

In my work as a Guardian Ad Litem, I became increasingly aware of the special needs of infants and toddlers. Realizing the critical nature of their needs, I developed an innovative program to address them. This program provided specialized advocacy on behalf of young children in foster care. During this time, I worked daily with early childhood experts including therapists, psychologists, and pediatricians. Coincidentally, I had just given birth to my third child. I had already parented two daughters successfully through their preschool years and assumed my husband and I had parenting pretty much mastered. Instead, I found it was interesting to be learning so much every day about infants and toddlers while I had one at home.

My son was about two years old when I had a particularly long, hard day at work. It was late when I arrived home, and I was exhausted. Although at first my little guy appeared happy to see me, within seconds he switched into an angry mode. He ran into me with his head down, nearly causing me to tumble over. I picked him up and he began hitting. This behavior was uncharacteristic of him. My first instinct was to scold him and put him to bed early, assuming he was tired. However, I knew this wasn't normal behavior, and I decided I would try to get to the bottom of it. I thought about his day—from his perspective. What did he not have that day that perhaps he really needed? I knew he counted on my coming home before dinner every night. His routine involved dinner with the whole family. Maybe he was just mad that I didn't appear when he expected. Drawing on what I had been learning from other professionals, I scooped him up in my arms, held him tight, and told him

Mommy was sorry for being gone so long. I told him I knew he missed me and I missed him too. Like a ball of wax, he melted into my embrace and rested his head on my shoulder. We sat together for a few minutes and then off he went, happily playing with his older sisters.

I was dumbfounded. He had been with his grandmother and his sisters in his own house all day. They had been to the park and eaten McDonald's for lunch, a treat which only Grandma allows. He had books read to him and a bath time with tub toys. Yet he still needed to be snuggled and reassured by his mom. What would have happened if I had simply scolded him and put him to bed early? I imagine his anger and behavior would have escalated into a full-blown temper tantrum.

This made me wonder what it is like for toddlers who find themselves in foster care after suffering abuse and neglect. Surely, their behavior would be out of whack too. What they desperately need is a relationship with one person who can see them through their emotional ups and downs. Children need to be able to count on someone to understand them, who will meet their needs. It is a vicious cycle. Trauma, fear, and anxiety impact behavior. This behavior can become difficult to manage and can result in foster parents seeking removal of children from their home. Additional changes in placement only fuel children's desperation.

Although behavior accounts for some of the placement changes young children experience, it is not the only reason multiple moves occur. Even young infants frequently move from home to home. "When a baby faces a change in placement, fragile new relationships with foster parents are severed, reinforcing feelings of abandonment and distrust. Even young babies are capable of grief when their relationships are disrupted" (Cohen and Youcha, 2004, p. 16). It is critical for infants and toddlers to experience a healthy attachment to an adult who is consistent, loving, and stable. When they are unable to develop this bond, they are at risk of having lifelong social and emotional problems.

Consider the plight of Thomas, who lived with four different families by the time he was five months old. Thomas was born into this world with wide eyes and a crown of black, curly hair. He and his mother, Shondra, left the hospital twenty-four hours after his birth. She walked out of the hospital into a ninety degree, muggy July day. Loaded with samples of baby formula and a small diaper bag, Thomas and Shondra boarded a bus that took them home to an apartment in a drug-infested neighborhood. She crossed the threshold into her sparsely furnished apartment and sweat immediately began to pour from her. She laid him on the old couch and disappeared into the adjoining bedroom, where a full size mattress occupied the floor. She collapsed into a deep sleep, waking two hours later to Thomas, who was screaming for his next bottle.

Shondra was exhausted from labor and delivery. She did not have family to help her. Her grandmother, who had recently died, raised her and her sisters. Her sisters drifted away, each lost in their own worlds of poverty and parenting. Shondra did not have groceries, air conditioning, or diapers. The next day, she and Thomas went to the grocery store to get the essentials. She spent her last $20 on diapers and boxes of macaroni and cheese.

Thomas was one month old when Shondra called Children's Services to report that she felt overwhelmed and could not take care of him. She was severely depressed and could hardly get out of bed. When a caseworker asked her about Thomas and his physical health, she replied that he was fine. He had never been to the doctor for any well-baby checks, but Shondra thought he was doing OK. He was little, but all babies were. Thomas went to live with his aunt while his mother was hospitalized for psychiatric care. His first doctor's appointment revealed low weight gain.

The doctor decided to re-check his weight weekly to see whether he would start gaining once he was in a more stable, caring environment. After caring for Thomas for three weeks, his aunt called the Children's Services caseworker and said she could no longer care for him. She also indicated that she didn't have time to attend his weight checks at the clinic. Although she had originally thought she could handle taking care of Thomas, she was increasingly unable to juggle him along with her own three children. She was a single mother and worked full-time. It was too much for her to manage on her own. Thomas was placed with a foster family. His foster parents had fostered dozens of children before Thomas and welcomed him with open arms. Their own children were grown and they doted on him. Thomas returned to the clinic for weekly weight checks and was gaining just enough to keep him from being diagnosed with Failure to Thrive. He had a problem with reflux, and so spit up regularly. His foster parents switched his formula at the doctor's request and his weight began to improve incrementally.

When Thomas was five months old, his foster father suffered a major heart attack. His foster mother spent every waking minute at the hospital while a babysitter cared for Thomas. When it became clear that his foster father's recovery would be long and hard, the foster parents requested that Thomas be moved to another home. Although they hated to see Thomas leave, they felt they just couldn't care for him while dealing with this medical crisis. Thomas was then moved to a second foster home, his fourth placement in less than six months.

Many families with young children experience crises that test their strength and functioning. Family illness, divorce, unemployment, or a spouse going off to war all impact families in a significant way, with many parents wondering at night how they will face the morning. However, most of these parents wouldn't dream of handing their children over to foster care while they try to deal with the crisis at hand. They would enlist the help of extended family, friends, or church members to help them instead.

Foster families are different. Foster children can be given back when it gets too difficult to care for them. At the end of the day, thousands of foster children go to bed without being firmly rooted in a family, despite how loving and well intended their foster parents are.

Through no fault of his own, Thomas was dealt a rough start to his journey through this world. In the past, we believed that babies didn't know the difference between one home and another. Because babies can't use words to tell us their fears, frustrations, and worries, we previously assumed that they didn't suffer from those emotions. The science of early childhood development has taught us differently.

The entire job of a baby is to learn about the world around them. It's impossible to do this job if the world keeps changing and the people in it disappear. When this happens, a child's growth and development is impaired. "Infants and toddlers who do not have an opportunity to form an attachment with a trusted adult (i.e. infants and toddlers who experience multiple foster homes) suffer, and their development can deteriorate, resulting in delays in cognition and learning, relationship dysfunction, and difficulty expressing emotions" (Cohen and Youcha, 2004, p. 17).

Thomas was learning that the world was a scary place. He could not depend on the same person to get him out of his crib in the morning. He wasn't sure who was going to come when he cried. Would anyone come at all? The world was teaching Thomas that people could not be counted on to stick around and meet his needs. It's difficult to unlearn these beliefs as children age, particularly when their lives remain in the hands of a foster care system that cannot guarantee much of anything.

Thomas' experience is not as unusual as you might think. Thomas' caseworker did everything possible to minimize the number of moves Thomas made. Knowing Thomas could not remain with his mother, the caseworker sought out relatives to care for him. When Thomas' aunt agreed, the caseworker offered daycare vouchers and financial assistance. Even so, this placement failed. The caseworker then relied on a foster family that could care for him. Although that was going well, the unexpected medical crisis rendered that family unable to keep him. The tragedy is in the long-term implications of these multiple moves. If Thomas continues to move from home to home, he will be more likely to experience difficulty in developing and maintaining healthy relationships with others as he grows. Sometimes children who have experienced profound abuse or neglect and have been deprived of a consistent, loving caregiver are diagnosed with Reactive Attachment Disorder, meaning they are unable to experience healthy emotional relationships with others. This impacts their ability to maintain placement in a foster family. Just when they begin to feel settled and too close to their foster family, they sabotage it. It is safer not to rely on anyone for anything. This doesn't go away as children age either, and impacts their ability to form good relationships with peers or potential life partners.

Thomas' second foster placement offered him stability for the first time in his short life. His foster mother did not work outside the home, which prevented him from having to make additional transitions to a new environment. Thomas was developmentally delayed and his weight increased, but only by ounces at a time. He did not babble or attempt to make any sounds other than crying. Thomas slept for an inordinate amount of time every day. It was as though he began choosing to disengage from life.

The routine and consistency he experienced in this foster home did wonders for him. After several weeks, he began to "wake up." He became curious about his surroundings and began to explore the world around him. His problems with reflux and vomiting lessened and he slowly continued gaining weight. He also began babbling and squealing and crying, all of which were welcomed from the baby who used to sleep all the time. His personality came to life, and he began thriving. "Attachment provides a protection against psychopathology by buffering children from the harmful, long-term effects of psychological trauma" (Fonargy, 2001). If Thomas had not experienced the safety, stability, and love this family offered, it is likely that he would have experienced behavior problems and academic problems when he reached preschool.

Although Thomas was thriving, his mother did not fare so well. She began smoking marijuana after her psychiatric hospitalization. She was evicted from her apartment. She moved from place to place, staying with friends whenever possible and at times living in homeless shelters. She was never able to change her lifestyle, and Thomas' foster family eventually adopted him.

Young children enter foster care needing a lot of help. They need stability and comfort. They need order and routine. They desperately need a healthy relationship with one loving and caring adult. This particular need is as basic as their need for food, water, and shelter. Their growth and future development will suffer if they lack this basic need. Yet this is the one thing foster care routinely cannot provide.

By the time Adam and Sarah arrived at their second foster home, they had experienced chronic domestic violence and had witnessed their parents' brutal beating of someone. They had endured separation from the adults they knew and experienced great loss as a result.

Adam and Sarah's foster parents had fostered less than a dozen children in the two years they had been licensed. Adam and Sarah were the youngest children ever placed in their home, and there were no other foster children living with this family at the time Adam and Sarah were in this home. The foster family was comprised of the foster parents, Chuck and Paula, and their fourteen-year-old biological daughter, Chelsea. Adam and Sarah went to a babysitter's home when both foster parents were working.

While Adam unpacked his garbage bags, he also unloaded his hostility. He challenged the foster parents with every request they made of him. When asked to put his dinner dishes in the sink, Adam threw them with such force they shattered against the tile floor. He refused to use the bathroom and instead urinated on the living room couch. Adam waged daily battles against his foster parents. They responded by being patient and firm. Despite their best efforts, his behavior continued.

While Adam's foster parents worked with him, Sarah spent time with Chelsea. They forged a loving relationship and Sarah enjoyed the doting she received from her new sister. Together they read stories, colored pictures, and played dolls.

Adam's behavior problems continued at the foster home and at the babysitter's house. Unaccustomed to being around other young children, Adam tended to lash out when he did not get his way. He frequently hit, kicked, and bit the other children, including his sister. Within two weeks, the babysitter refused to allow Adam back into her home.

The foster parents searched for another childcare setting for Adam and Sarah for the two days each week that Paula worked. They arranged childcare at a center, hoping that the staff there would be better able to manage Adam's behavior. On the first day at the new center, Adam bit a staff member. Each day, Paula or Chuck was called to come and retrieve Adam, as he was out of control.

Adam was referred for therapy at a counseling center across town, near his first foster home. It would be a forty-minute drive for his new family.

At the request of the foster parents Lisa, the caseworker, re-referred Adam for services at a center closer to his new foster home. Shortly thereafter, Adam completed an intake appointment for play therapy. He was assigned a therapist. He had one session with this individual before she resigned from her job. Then, he was put on a waiting list for a new therapist. In the meantime, Adam was expelled from the childcare center. He was disruptive and his behavior posed a risk to the other children. Paula considered quitting her job, but she enjoyed it, and the family needed her salary to maintain their lifestyle.

In the meantime, Sarah was steadily becoming comfortable in her new foster home. She cried less and was more open to affection from her older foster sister and her foster parents. She participated in activities at the childcare center and seemed to enjoy them.

Chuck and Paula faced a tough choice. They could request that Adam be moved to a new home or Paula could quit her job. After much consideration, they asked for Adam's removal. They were willing to keep his sister, but decided they just couldn't manage him.

Lisa faced a tough choice as well. Should Adam and Sarah be moved together or separated? Sarah was doing so well with her foster family. She had settled in and appeared to have formed good relationships with them. Even so, how would the separation from her brother affect her? On the other hand, Sarah was often on the receiving end of Adam's anger. He would frequently kick her or push her down. Would Adam make more progress if he were placed in a home without other children, where foster parents could focus only on him?

The decision was made to move Adam. Sarah would stay. Chuck and Paula sat down with Adam one night and told him he would be leaving their home and going to live with a new family. They explained that he needed help learning how to behave better and that they could not help him. They told him a new family would be able to do a better job taking care of him. They told him that though Sarah was not going to be leaving with him, he could still come and visit Sarah. Adam sat and listened. When his foster parents asked him if he had any questions, he had only one thing to say.

"I hate you."

CHAPTER 5

A Fork in the Road

ADAM'S STORMY EYES HINTED at the madness that was brewing inside of him. Adam lived in an unpredictable world and felt no control over anything. The world had completely overwhelmed this little boy. Chaos and uncertainty had become his life.

Let's think about what the world had taught Adam thus far. He learned from watching his parents that people hurt each other. He learned that he could never know for sure what the next day would bring. Finally, he learned that people could give him away. How will he unlearn all of this if he does not have healthy relationships with people who can teach him differently?

All of us learn about relationships through important people in our lives. As children, we learned from our parents. Hopefully, our parents taught us right from wrong and disciplined us with love when necessary. We learned that we belonged to a family and we had a place in this world.

As adults, we continue learning as we grow in relationships with friends and family. Through our own imperfections, people who love us teach us the depth of forgiveness. Their support during difficulties we face connects us and helps sustain us while we make our life's journey. Nearly everything we learn and all of our emotional growth happens in our relationships with other people.

Adam had two things when he left the foster home he had shared with his sister, and neither one included a healthy relationship with anyone. He had a caseworker he saw, usually during a crisis, and two bags of clothes and toys. That's it.

From his perspective, can you begin to understand how out of control he must have felt? Wouldn't it then make sense that his behavior would be out of control as well? Without the skills to articulate in words how he felt, how else could he portray the utter chaos of his life?

Judging from his behavior, Adam had plenty to say about what was happening. When Lisa arrived, Adam refused to get in the car. He screamed and cried. Eventually she wrestled him into his booster seat and employed the use of child safety locks on the doors. It was a good thing she did, because within minutes Adam attempted to open the car door. It was a long thirty-minute drive to Adam's new foster home.

Imagine this car traveling down the road. Suppose it comes to a fork and is forced down one path or another. Foster homes sit at the end of each path. One home houses a family who is loving, experienced, and truly dedicated to children. At the end of the other path lives a family who sees a foster child and immediately sees a board rate, or money the government will pay to care for a foster child. Imagine you are the child in the backseat of this car. The cold seat matches the cold fear gripping your heart. You have no idea where the car will take you. All you know is that the driver will drop you off in a strange place with people you have never seen before. The car will vanish, along with the driver, who is one of the only familiar sights in your life.

Is your heart pounding yet? Do you have a sick feeling in the pit of your stomach? Have you ever gone on vacation and stayed at the home of friends or distant relatives? Despite your level of comfort with these people, it is sometimes awkward to share their home. Maybe you sit down to dinner and find that no matter how hard you try, you can't seem to choke down the meal that was made especially for you. Not wanting to hurt your hosts' feelings, you smile politely and try to push the food around on your plate, making it look like you have eaten something. Later you run bath water and the pipes make a terrible noise. You stop suddenly. Did you break something? Did a pipe burst? This is the bathroom you were supposed to use, right?

No matter how welcoming your hosts are, oftentimes worries arise, reminding you that you are a guest in someone's home. Even though you are not staying with strangers, you may look forward to returning to the comfort of your own home, where you can fix your own meals and go about your daily business without worrying you have done something wrong. But if you are a foster child like Adam, you have no home to return to.

Making his way to his new foster home, Adam had no idea where he would be taken, or to what kind of people he would be delivered. It would be nice if the system could guarantee that Adam will live in a foster home where he would be loved, nurtured, and protected. This may or may not happen.

Many foster homes are safe havens for children who have been abused and neglected. Even so, far too many foster parents lack the skills and fail to receive the support necessary to help kids like Adam. Finally, there are foster homes that are indifferent to children or worse, abusive and neglectful.

Adam is again at a critical juncture in his young life. Depending on where the car will take him, he may be offered the opportunity to heal and grow. He may find himself in a home that will provide him the first consistency and stability he has ever known. He may be lucky enough to land in the arms of foster parents who are able to absorb his anger and fear and hold him steady while he learns new ways of living. He may thrive under the care and love of adults dedicated to giving him his first chance at a childhood. He may meet the people who will save his life.

It is also possible that he may walk through the front door of a foster home and sit quietly on a couch while his new foster mother asks his caseworker a barrage of questions. "When do I get a clothing voucher for him? What do you mean he's not in preschool? How am I supposed to go to work if he didn't come with childcare vouchers? I told your agency I don't do bed wetters." Adam may be shown to a small bedroom with two sets of bunk beds. Maybe there are no curtains on the windows and no dressers. Clothes are simply left on the floor. He may share this small bedroom with three other foster kids. Down the hall, the foster parents' two biological children may enjoy their own bedrooms, decorated to the hilt in character themes of their choice. Foster care rules require beds, but Adam may or may not have bed linens.

Adam may be one of the thousands of children who will be abused in foster care this year. His story may unfold like that of five-year-old Haley, a young girl placed in foster care after suffering severe physical abuse at the hands of her mother. Haley frequently wet the bed at night and was living with a foster family when she arrived at preschool one morning quiet and withdrawn. When a purple crayon slipped from her little fingers and fell to the floor, she bent down to retrieve it, revealing bruises on her lower back. The teacher gently pulled her aside and asked her how she got the bruises. Tears filled Haley's eyes as she explained that she had wet the bed two nights earlier, and her foster mother had hit her because of it. At the end of the morning, Haley's classmates were dismissed into the waiting embraces of their parents, grandparents, or babysitters. Haley sat in the nurse's office, waiting for her caseworker to come and take her to a new home.

Less likely, but nevertheless a possibility, Adam may join the ranks of Marcus Fiesel. He may become one of the dozens of children murdered at the hands of his foster parents. Like Marcus Fiesel, foster care became a death sentence for nine-month-old Ebony. After a bout of incessant crying, Ebony's foster father shook her to death in a fit of rage. He was subsequently sentenced to five years in prison. Although infants and toddlers are at greatest risk, homicide of foster children occurs at all ages.

More likely than either of the above scenarios, Adam will join the thousands of foster children who move from foster home to foster home without any hope of finding a permanent family. Emotionally scarred and behaviorally challenged, children like Adam struggle to find a place to belong. They lack healthy relationships with caregivers, and oftentimes, the support of professionals who are skilled at helping them. As these children age, their problems grow while their chances of ever finding a family to love them diminish.

If Adam stays on the path of disrupted foster placements, he will certainly experience a downward spiral that will become increasingly difficult to stop as he ages. Foster children like Adam who move from home to home find themselves in dire straights. With each disruption, foster children become a little more lost and a little less likely to find a family to love them and help them.

As Adam gets older and starts school, a new host of problems will likely begin. Thanks to his early life experiences, the structure and routine of school will be difficult for Adam to manage. When a child knows chaos more than stability, he or she tends to perpetuate that chaos which has become familiar. Sometimes the only control children like Adam have is to behave so uncontrollably that the entire class is disrupted. Even if Adam is able to attend school with some success, his school will change each time he changes foster homes. Each time foster children are enrolled in a new school, there are new rules to master, new classmates to meet, and new cultures to navigate.

Suppose ten years pass. As a child who has grown up in the system, Adam will be more likely to drop out of high school. He may live in group homes or other facilities and will begin taking classes to learn how to function in the world as an adult. On his eighteenth birthday, he legally becomes an adult and will be fully responsible for himself in this world without any family or support to fall back on. He will be more likely than other children to engage in criminal activity. He may end up like twenty-year-old Derrick. Derrick came into foster care at the age of four. He bounced between foster care and failed reunification attempts with his biological mother. He was placed in multiple group homes as a teenager, but always ran away, back to a life on the streets. He walked away from the system at eighteen with no family, no place to live, no source of income, and no high school degree. Life on the streets was hard for him. He was bone thin and exhausted most of the time.

Derrick resurfaced at age nineteen. He had been incarcerated for aggravated robbery and theft. Interestingly enough, Derrick had his first experience with structure and routine inside the four walls of his jail cell. For the first time in years, he could count on regular meals.

Although Adam can count on regular meals, he can't count on much more. The future does not look good for Adam. Riding along in his caseworker's car, he really has no idea what will happen to him next. Is it any wonder that he tried to jump out?

Lisa continued on until she came to the address she was looking for. Directions to the new foster home led to the outskirts of town, and down a country road to a long gravel driveway. A two-story white house with green shutters was to her left, and a lake complete with a family of ducks was to the right. Two old, wooden rocking chairs sat on the large front porch, facing the lake across the road. An older couple occupied the chairs and stood up when they saw the caseworker's car approach.

Lisa exited the car and walked around to the other side to help Adam climb out of his booster seat. She opened his car door and coaxed him out. He refused to come. She pleaded with him, to no avail. Not knowing what to do, she looked helplessly at his new foster parents, who had walked over to the car to greet them.

The foster father spoke first. "You must be Adam. I'm Pop, and this is Nana. We've been waiting for you. We're happy you've come to stay with us." Adam ignored him entirely and buried his face in his crossed arms. Undaunted, the foster father kept talking. "You know, it's almost supper time for the horses. You came just in time. I was hoping you would help me feed them."

Adam's head tilted and one eye peeked out from underneath his shaggy brown hair. The caseworker bent down to him, still fastened in his seat. "Adam, why don't you take a look at the horses? I'll wait here for you until you come back."

Adam looked up to the caseworker then back to this stranger. Lisa mentioned that Adam had never seen farm animals before. Pop spoke up. "We have lots of animals around here. The horses are out back. Spencer usually hangs right around the fence. He likes to be petted. How would you like to meet him?"

Adam pondered the offer and slowly climbed out of the car. Pop extended his hand and offered it to Adam. Adam backed away and stuffed his tiny clenched fists into the pockets of his Scooby-Doo shorts. Nevertheless, Adam followed him across the field.

Lisa and Nana climbed a handful of steps that led to the front porch, where they sat and went over his history. She briefly described his behavior problems and indicated that he did not get along well with other children. Nana smiled and said this would not be a problem. She and her husband had four grown children. No other children lived with them. Nana did not have a job outside the home. Childcare was not necessary.

They discussed Adam's violent outbursts and his inability to follow directions. Nana assured the caseworker that they had fostered many children in the past with the same history, and she felt confident that she and her husband could manage Adam as well.

Twenty minutes later Adam and Pop returned to the kitchen where the caseworker and foster mother were meeting. The foster parents asked Adam if he would like to see where he would be sleeping. The four of them walked upstairs and down a hallway that led to his bedroom. By sheer coincidence, a Scooby-Doo comforter covered the bed. The hint of a smile played across Adam's face.

Soon the caseworker departed, telling Adam that she would be back to check on him another day. Adam didn't speak. He simply sat stone-faced and stared at her.

Several weeks passed before Lisa returned to the foster home to see how Adam was adjusting. When she arrived, Adam was racing his toy cars across the front porch. Nana sat in a nearby rocking chair. Adam continued playing while the two adults talked.

The first month in Adam's new home was not without problems. Adam woke the first morning in his new bed screaming. In ragged breaths, he insisted that someone was coming to kill him. He wouldn't allow his foster parents to touch him. He ran out of his bedroom and down the stairs, determined to get out of the house and away from them. His foster parents stood by calmly while he raged. In time, he settled down and all at once, the crying stopped.

It was not uncommon for Adam to wake during the night screaming. He laid in bed, terrified, not awake, but not asleep either. During these times, Nana would come to his room and sit on his bed, talking to him in a soothing voice, attempting to calm him. Eventually he would fall back asleep. After the first couple of weeks, the night terrors became shorter and his sleep was more peaceful.

Although he seemed to be experiencing some peace when he slept, he certainly did not experience much of that during the day. Neither did his foster parents. Adam had endless energy, and bounced around the house going from room to room, often leaving a mess in his wake. He loved to play with puzzles. However, he would only work on one for just moments before he was onto another activity. Nana worked hard at redirecting him and working alongside him, but it was exhausting. When it was time to clean up, Adam often refused to help.

One day while Nana was on the phone, Adam quietly slipped into the computer room and used scissors to cut the cords of the family computer and printer. When the foster parents sat Adam down to discuss this, he adamantly refused to admit that he did it. Lying was routine for Adam. The foster parents were furious. Despite their anger and frustration, they remained committed to taking care of Adam. While they could provide a stable home for him, he needed more help than they alone could give.

Soon after this experience, Adam's long-awaited referral for therapy came through. Fortunately for Adam and his foster parents, Mary, the therapist assigned, was an experienced clinician who had worked with children like Adam for many years. Adam's weekly therapy appointment proved to be an anchor that helped Adam and his foster parents weather the storms of Adam's behavior. Mary worked with him to reduce his anxiety and make sense of the story of his life. Equally as important, Mary supported Pop and Nana, helped them understand Adam's behavior, and offered helpful suggestions in dealing with it.

At Mary's suggestion, Nana began and ended each day by reading Adam a story while they sat on the front porch. At first, she sat in a rocking chair and Adam looked over her shoulder. They started with short books, as Adam's attention span didn't last for more than a couple of minutes. In time, Adam was able to handle longer books. He slowly moved from standing behind her to standing next to her. Eventually, he accepted her invitation to climb up on her lap.

Adam's gradual ability to accept the nurturing his foster mother offered him was critical in helping him heal. Adam had missed out on many important early life experiences. As an infant and toddler of two violent, drug-abusing parents, he did not have an adult who was focused on meeting his physical and emotional needs. He did not experience crucial life-experiences, such as healthy physical and nurturing contact. He did not learn how to engage with an adult in a loving way.

Before he could have a loving and healthy relationship with an adult, he first would need to learn that adults could be trusted to meet his needs. For a child like Adam, this trust can be a long time coming. The emotional damage done to Adam did not occur overnight, and it would take time to undo.

As the daily rocking chair time continued, Adam began to depend on this special time with Nana. In time, he was captivated by the stories unfolding on the pages his foster mother read to him. His imagination was unleashed as he listened to tales of magic and wonder.

Sometimes, Adam didn't want a story. Sometimes he just wanted to cuddle up into her lap and soak up the magic of having someone hold him, love him, and protect him. Nana understood that he needed this time to be held and cuddled. In order for Adam to improve his behavior and progress in his development, he first had to be offered the opportunity to go backwards in his development and enjoy a more infantile relationship with his foster parents. Once this building block was in place, the foundation of a happy childhood was one step closer to being complete.

While Mary played a crucial role in helping him cope with his feelings and understand them, her work with his foster parents was critical. Adam was a little boy who demanded a tremendous amount of attention and oversight, but who gave little in return. There were many days when he was impossibly difficult to like, though they loved him. Mary encouraged his foster parents to hang in there. She wisely offered them the opportunity to call her and vent when they needed to. She listened to their struggles without judging them or Adam, and gently reminded them of the progress Adam had made, and how much of a difference they had made in his life. Those phone conversations always ended with the foster parents feeling shored up and ready for another day.

Together, Mary, Pop, and Nana made a very powerful team. The combination of therapy and stability began to strengthen Adam and repair damage done to him early on. These people began to build the first solid foundation Adam had experienced in his life.

Adam benefited greatly by being the only child in his foster home. The lack of commotion caused by several children living under one roof was good for him. Because Adam was the only child in this home, he was not faced with negotiating peer interaction. He did not have to share toys or more importantly, the time and attention of his foster parents. Although these are necessary skills, it was helpful for Adam to be able to learn how to function in a healthy family unit before learning these other skills.

Life had been very hard for Adam. The break he got from living in this situation was one he very much needed. Before he could do the hard work of learning how to function in this world without aggression and violence, he had to first experience some sense of calm.

While Adam was settling into his foster home, Sarah remained with Chuck and Paula, along with Chelsea. Sarah celebrated her third birthday with this family, and by then, had lived in their home for nearly one third of her life. For several months after Adam's separation from Sarah, there was no communication between the two children. Adam asked repeatedly about Sarah and wanted to see her. Chuck and Paula reported that Sarah cried and was scared when they talked to her about going to see her brother. For these reasons, the caseworker didn't initiate contact between the children.

Adam continued attending weekly therapy and in his sessions, he began to talk more and more about Sarah. Mary believed that it was in Adam's best interest to reconnect with his sister. Too often people, even siblings, disappear from children's lives without explanation. In the meantime, Sarah's foster parents did not want Sarah exposed to her brother. They were convinced that he would upset her. Trusting the therapist's assessment, Lisa agreed to a visit between Adam and Sarah. This visit occurred under the guidance of the therapist in her office.

The day arrived for the long-awaited reunion between Sarah and Adam. As promised, each set of foster parents brought the children to the therapist's office for the visit. While Adam seemed happy to see Sarah, she looked confused. After re-introducing the children to each other, Mary facilitated their play and helped them negotiate their interaction. At the close of the visit, the children hugged and parted ways. Visits continued in Mary's office once each week. They both began looking forward to their time together. After a month of visits, Pop and Nana asked permission to have Sarah spend a weekend at their home. Sarah's foster parents did not want her to go. Even though visits had gone well between Adam and Sarah, Chuck and Paula did not want to extend contact between the children. Sarah had become a part of their family, and they had no interest in introducing any other idea of family to her. Again, with Mary's recommendation, Sarah began spending every other weekend with Adam in his foster home.

Even though they were finally on the right track, they were far from getting where they needed to be. Although their everyday life was running smoothly, their future was still uncertain, and was in the hands of the court. The Juvenile Court magistrate who oversaw their case and ordered their initial placement in foster care was in the driver's seat.

A year had passed since Adam and Sarah's mom and dad had beaten and robbed their acquaintance. Their parents had remained in jail awaiting their own trials in criminal court. Even so, they still had rights to Adam and Sarah, such as the right to consent or not to the children getting haircuts and the right to choose their religious upbringing.

The parents' criminal trial concluded a year after the children's removal from their care. They were each sentenced to serve eight years in prison. They would not be able available to raise their kids.

Adam and Sarah needed a permanent home. They could not stay in foster care as wards of the state forever. Decisions about their future needed to be made. The attorney representing Children's Services filed a motion on behalf of the caseworker in juvenile court for termination of parental rights. In essence, termination of parental rights is the death of a biological family as a family unit. The parents received this motion while incarcerated and were informed of their right to be present at the trial and to be represented by a public defender. Lisa had written to them several times over the past year to inquire about other family members who could take Adam and Sarah. Each time she asked, the parents told her no relatives were available.

On the day of the permanent custody trial, the parents appeared in handcuffs and shackles. The parents' criminal behavior and subsequent sentencing tied their legal hands much like the handcuffs they wore. They would never be permitted to raise their children. Sobbing, Adam's mother told the magistrate she had an aunt who was willing to take the children. The magistrate postponed the trial and ordered the caseworker to investigate the relative for possible placement.

In the meantime, Adam and Sarah were more settled than they had ever been in their foster homes. They continued spending weekends together in Adam's foster home. Under the watchful eye of Nana and Pop, the visits went well. Adam and Sarah spent time playing together. Pop took them fishing and they roamed around the farm, playing hide and seek. Although Sarah was happy to spend this time with Adam, she was also happy to return to her foster home.

Lisa arrived at one of these sibling visits to talk to Adam and Sarah about their great Aunt Theresa. As delicately as she could, she asked the children whether they knew their mom's Aunt Theresa. Sarah had no idea what the caseworker was talking about and she continued playing with her toy kitchen and plastic food. Adam was a little more thoughtful, but he had nothing to say about his "real mom" or anyone related to her.

The caseworker contacted Aunt Theresa and scheduled a time to visit in her home. She lived in a small apartment just twenty minutes from Lisa's office. Lisa spent an hour talking with Aunt Theresa, who gave the following story.

Theresa was the maternal great aunt to Adam and Sarah. She knew the children were in foster care, and had been for quite some time. She said she had tried to find out more about where they were and how to get them, but said she didn't know who to call or what to do. She told the caseworker of her niece's troubled childhood and how she tried to help her, but was busy trying to raise her kids on her own. She was interested in beginning visitation with the children with the intention of seeking legal custody of both of them.

Aunt Theresa was single and lived in a two-bedroom apartment with her grown daughter, age twenty-six. Her three grandchildren, ages two, three, and seven spent each weekend with her. She was a nursing assistant and worked nights at a retirement home. She was off work on the weekends.

Lisa ran a criminal background check, which showed a theft charge from four years earlier, as well as a charge for passing bad checks. When Lisa called her on the phone to discuss her findings, Aunt Theresa stated she was desperate at the time and couldn't make ends meet. She said she understood that what she had done was wrong and that she had learned from this mistake. She did not have a history with Children's Services. She indicated that her grown daughter would move out of the apartment to allow space for Adam and Sarah. Aunt Theresa would need childcare assistance if Adam and Sarah came to live with her.

The caseworker reported these findings to the court and recommended that Aunt Theresa should file for custody, become a legal party to the case, and present testimony as to why it would be in the children's best interests to live with her. Against this, the magistrate ordered weekend visitation for Adam and Sarah with Aunt Theresa. The trial for permanent custody was set out for three months. If the visits did not go well and relative placement would not be possible, the trial to terminate the parent's rights to the children would occur at that time.

At Lisa's request, Adam's therapist made every effort to contact Aunt Theresa and invite her to visit with both children in her office prior to their first weekend visit. She was unable to attend any therapy sessions because she had begun working extra hours at the retirement home and could not make it to the counseling center.

The foster parents were left to explain to the children that they would be spending the weekend with Aunt Theresa. Lisa retrieved both Adam and

Sarah from their foster homes and took them to the aunt's apartment on a Friday afternoon. Aunt Theresa answered the door and gushed over how darling both Adam and Sarah were. She bent down, looked Sarah directly in the eye, and told her how much she looked like her mom. Sarah looked confused and immediately began to cry. Adam entered the apartment and darted from room to room. Frenzied, he checked out the space and all it held. The caseworker handed over their duffle bags, full of their favorite books, stuffed animals, and clothes. It was not long before Lisa left, promising the children that she would be back on Monday morning to take them to their foster homes.

Bright and early on Monday morning, Lisa arrived at Aunt Theresa's home. When Aunt Theresa opened the door, she pulled Lisa inside and gave her an earful. It was obvious by the anxious look on her face that something was wrong. She screeched that Adam could not be controlled. She said he was wild and had bounced around the apartment non-stop. He was rude, and mean, and had hit her when she tried to send him to bed early the night before. Sarah had cried off and on the whole weekend over the slightest frustration, like having trouble putting on her winter coat. Aunt Theresa decided she was not up for the task of raising them. They would be too much to manage.

When Adam and Sarah caught sight of Lisa standing at the door, they scrambled to her. They couldn't get out of the apartment fast enough, and when they were finally loaded into the caseworker's car, they both fell fast asleep.

Both sets of foster parents reported that it took nearly a week before Adam and Sarah settled back into their respective homes. Adam returned to his behaviors of lying and aggression. Sarah was whiney and demanding, easily frustrated and prone to temper tantrums.

Three months passed and the date for the permanent custody trial arrived. The mother's attorney failed to make arrangements to have her transferred from prison to the permanent custody trial. Because she had a right to attend, the case was postponed. Another four months passed before the next trial date was available and all attorneys had a mutual date clear on their calendars.

While a healthy relationship between Adam and Sarah developed, tensions between the two sets of foster parents grew. Decisions regarding where the children would ultimately resided were pending. If they were freed for adoption, should they be adopted together or separately? Sarah's foster parents desperately wanted to adopt her, but not Adam. Although they felt they were too old to adopt, Nana and Pop had witnessed the growth in relationship between the kids and felt strongly that they should grow up together.

One day Lisa arrived at Sarah's foster home to complete her monthly home visit, and as she approached the front door, she heard Paula and Chuck screaming at each other. She tentatively rang the bell and the door swung open. As Chuck stormed out, Paula dissolved into tears and informed the caseworker that she and her husband would be separating. She asked the caseworker how this would impact her ability to eventually adopt Sarah. Lisa responded that she wasn't sure, as no decisions had been made regarding placing Adam and Sarah together in an adoptive home. Paula became irate and stated if she could not adopt Sarah, then she wanted her out that day.

The caseworker tried to calm her, but it was no use. The foster mother became so distraught that Lisa was unsure whether Sarah would be safe in her home that night. The caseworker suggested that Sarah stay with Adam's foster family for a few nights so that Chuck and Paula could try to work through their difficulties. Paula agreed and packed some of Sarah's things while the caseworker made arrangements with Adam's foster family for Sarah to stay for a few days.

CHAPTER 6

The Politics of
Child Welfare

ARAH SENSED THAT SOMETHING big was happening, as she watched
her foster father storm out of the house and heard her foster mother's
desperate demands about adopting her. After the arrangements had
been made, Sarah hugged her crying fourteen-year-old foster sister good-bye
and dutifully got into the car.

She sat in the backseat of Lisa's car, quiet as a mouse. It was dark
when Lisa arrived at Adam's foster home with Sarah in tow. The moon
hung low and crickets chirped their welcome as Lisa knocked on the door.
Soon the sound of Adam's feet could be heard running to the door, and
as he opened it, both Lisa and Sarah were wrapped in the cool air of the
peaceful country home.

Nana was finishing up the dinner dishes while Pop and Adam played a
board game on the living room floor. Nana called out hello and came into the
living room, drying her hands on a dishtowel. She took one look at Sarah,

standing still in the doorway, and bent down to hug her. As she scooped her up, Sarah nestled her head into the foster mother's neck and began to cry, her little arms clinging to the woman who held her while her tears were unleashed. While Sarah poured out her grief, the caseworker sat with Adam and Pop while they played Chutes and Ladders.

By the time Lisa left, Sarah had settled down. Adam and Pop continued their games while Sarah cuddled on Nana's lap. The sight of the four of them gave no hint of anything less than a family enjoying dinner together after a typical weekday. However, this was anything but a typical family. Rather than bloodlines connecting them, a government system, run by bureaucrats, had connected them together. The same government system could separate them at any moment, without warning.

Later that week, the caseworker learned that Sarah's foster family was dealing with their own family crises. Chuck and Paula had separated and the father had moved out of the family's home. Paula was distraught over the turn of events, and had been hospitalized for severe anxiety and depression. Sarah's former foster sister, Chelsea, had moved into a two-bedroom apartment with her father. It was not in Sarah's best interest to return to that family, despite the fact that they had been her family for over a year.

As expected, Adam had some trouble adjusting to sharing his home and his foster parents with his little sister. He enjoyed her weekend visits, but her living on his turf all the time was an entirely different story. Some of Adam's old behaviors returned. He fought with Sarah over books and toys and pushed her down once when he found her playing with his favorite cars. Nana and Pop patiently handled each flare-up as it occurred.

Adam's therapist had continued working with Adam weekly, and was aware that Sarah had joined him in his foster home. She talked frequently with Nana during the week, and offered support and suggestions with helping the family adjust to the change in their home. Through this process, it became apparent that Adam really struggled with sharing "his" Pop and Nana. Both Pop and Nana arranged to spend some quality time with Adam alone each day, and slowly his behavior problems dissolved.

One night after Pop and Nana had tucked Adam and Sarah into bed, the headlines of the nightly news caught their eyes and made their hearts skip a beat. Three-year-old Marcus Fiesel had been reported missing nearly two weeks earlier. The evening news announced the arrest of his foster parents in conjunction with his murder. Pop and Nana were horrified as they learned of the torturous death little Marcus had suffered.

They climbed the stairs to bed and paused at the doorways of Adam and Sarah's bedrooms. They watched the children sleeping soundly. Adam's Scooby-Doo comforter, which prompted the first smile they saw, was tucked up under his chin, his arm dangling over the side of the bed and one foot sticking out from under the covers. In the room next door, Sarah's breathing was quiet, her small chest moving up and down as each breath made its way in and out of her little body. She looked as peaceful as an angel, and Nana and Pop whispered a silent prayer of thanks for the little girl who had come into their home.

Although the children slept well, Nana and Pop didn't sleep much. They tossed and turned all night. Like Liz and David Carroll, who were charged with Marcus' murder, they were licensed through Lifeway for Youth. They did not personally know the Carrolls, but Nana and Pop had gone through the same classes as they did. They underwent the same training and licensing process. In a different turn of events, Adam or Sarah could have been placed with the Carrolls, and Marcus could have come to them.

Bright and early the next morning, the phone rang. A steady stream of callers continued throughout the day. The Lifeway caseworker called to say he needed to make a home visit by the end of the week. Lisa called to schedule a home visit within seventy-two hours. Other foster parents they had befriended called as well to discuss the news and ponder what would happen next.

When Marcus was reported missing in the park, the media frenzy began. Approximately thirteen days passed between when he was initially reported missing and when the details of his death emerged. Each of these thirteen days brought new details to light about his placement with the Carrolls and their history as foster parents. A picture of Marcus, innocence shining from his blue eyes as he clasped his hands in front of his mouth, was everywhere.

Always looking for new angles on the story, the media began reporting on the foster care system as a whole, and on how it works. Media coverage continued incessantly. Before this constant news coverage, people in the general public were lulled into the misconception that foster care is a storybook ending to a child's life of trauma. Every day the media painted pictures that distorted this view. It was as though the community was waking up from a dream to the frightening realities children face when they are placed in foster care.

In the course of those thirteen days, my co-workers and I had many conversations about Marcus and what may have happened to him. He had been missing for over a week. It seemed as if he had just vanished from the park, though no one but Liz Carroll ever reported him being in the park on that August day. Even the police dogs could not pick up his trail. As much as my co-workers and I didn't want to believe it, many of us feared that his foster mother or father had killed him in a fit of rage and was trying to cover his murder. Every day we meet parents who "lose it" and beat their children severely. Our work with children forces us to face the reality that people do brutal things to kids. Although we hope for the best, we realize the worst is also a possibility.

Although my co-workers and I were not strangers to this ugliness, none of us would have imagined that Marcus spent his last day on this earth urine-soaked, hungry, sweating, and bound by a blanket and packing tape in a hot closet. We would have never imagined that his little body, with his bright blue eyes and chubby toddler hands, had been doused with gasoline, set on fire, and then dumped into the river. These horrific details gripped the hearts of people in the community around Marcus. It seemed like wherever I went, people were talking about Marcus and the foster care system.

I come from a big family with a handful of sports fanatics, including my husband. I have to admit I never quite understood what was accomplished by yelling at the TV during a football game. The emotion with which some people follow their favorite sports teams is lost on me. They get incensed over a bad call by the referee and complain bitterly about the unfairness of it all. They yell instructions to the players from the comfort of their own homes, thinking that somehow this may lead to the outcome they desire. Their attempts at influencing the game are futile. It doesn't matter. Somehow behaving in this manner makes them feel better.

Being a GAL at the time Marcus died put me on the receiving end of opinions shared by everyone, from my closest friends to the receptionist at my doctor's office. People had strong feelings about Marcus. Fueled by shock and anger, they demanded instant change in the foster care system along with changes in laws that govern children and license foster families.

Listening to people share their thoughts and feelings about Marcus' story was a little bit like watching fans respond to a football game that has not gone well, although in this game, Marcus had lost his life. I was a receiver on the field, catching all the heat of people's outrage. I knew if they did more than coach from the sidelines, these people would be the ones who could help kids like Marcus win at the game of life.

People had many suggestions about what should be done immediately to hold the professionals involved accountable, and to save the foster children who resided in Lifeway Foster Homes. Let's look closely at their suggestions and compare them to the fans shouting instructions at players and coaches on the field.

Many in Marcus' community wanted Lifeway shut down and all children removed from these homes. If Lifeway personnel could license the Carrolls, certainly they shouldn't be in the business of providing foster homes for children. Strangers who shed tears over Marcus' death may have felt better if this happened. However, where would all the kids go? Back to mothers who choose to have relationships with sexual offenders who prey on their children? Back to the parents who are incarcerated because of drug trafficking? Back to the parents who had beaten them within an inch of their lives? What would happen to kids like Adam and Sarah, whose Lifeway foster parents loved them as if they were their own?

Child welfare professionals choose to do a difficult job that most of us would not consider. It is not easy to be in the midst of a child's pain and suffering, and a family's dysfunction. Even so, people demanded that Marcus' team of caseworkers be fired for their bitter failure to protect him. Who will replace them? People are not lining up to do this low-paying job that is emotionally taxing and frequently dangerous.

People further demanded change in the rules of the game, or the foster care laws. Changes are needed, but will the rules prevent the players, or children, from getting hurt in a game they never wanted to play? Tougher game rules may make the game safer, but when push comes to shove, there are no guarantees that children will escape unharmed.

We fans of children were suddenly thrust into watching a game unfold that we never wanted to see. Whether we wanted to or not, we could not avoid watching. It was everywhere. At the fitness center, every television was tuned to the various news stations, all reporting on Marcus. In restaurants across town, from pizza places to sports bars, at least one channel was tuned to the incessant coverage of Marcus' story. For months, news coverage didn't let up. Every time I managed to put it out of my mind, the media was there to put it right back in. So we stood in the stands, helpless, shouting out to anyone who would listen that something must be done.

For Marcus, the game was over. But for thousands of children like Marcus, the game is still on, with the stands empty and very few people willing to get in the game.

Local government officials took this opportunity to respond to the crowds, promising they had the answers. They proposed changes in laws and initiated processes that would provide further oversight of foster parents. Marcus' death revealed a large hole in the safety net in place to monitor foster parents in regards to criminal behavior.

Marcus had been living with the Carrolls for about one month when violence erupted between his foster parents and the police were called to their home. During this incident, David allegedly threw a knife at a microwave in the family's kitchen and punched holes in the walls. When the police arrived at the home, David ran upstairs and threatened to kill himself. He was arrested and charged with domestic violence. This case was mediated outside of a courtroom. In an agreement between Liz and David, David agreed not to drink alcohol while taking Depakote, an anti-depressant (Justice for Marcus, Special Section). His children later reported to Children's Services caseworkers that their father had held a knife to their mother's throat and threatened to kill her. Foster care laws required David or Liz to report his arrest to Marcus' Lifeway caseworker. They did not.

Foster care laws require complete background checks on foster parents prior to licensing. After initial licensing, checks are typically run once a year or every other year. David Carroll's arrest and subsequent charge of domestic violence would not have been discovered for at least six months after it occurred, unless the foster parents themselves reported it.

After Marcus' death, politicians proposed that Children's Services reveal all names of foster parents and their social security numbers in order to conduct daily background checks. Foster parents balked at this, in part because of a recent breach in the county system that failed to protect identity information for thousands of residents in the county. There was no plan identified for who would be responsible for running the daily checks, for where the information would be stored day to day, or for who would protect this information. Adam and Sarah's foster parents were hesitant to allow their information to be floating around indefinitely without a clear plan as to how it would be protected. I didn't blame them. Though, at the same time, I was a fan of frequent background checks.

Rick Roberts, Director of the Hamilton County Job and Family Services Agency, backed by county commissioners, stated publicly that children placed with foster parents who did not complete a background check within thirty days would be removed from those foster homes and placed elsewhere. While this directive may have made people in the general public feel better, it was not possible. The county commissioners and the agency director did not have the authority to demand that the children be removed. Only juvenile court judges or magistrates could authorize the removal of a child.

Although all Hamilton County foster parents had completed background checks when they were initially licensed, they were run again following Marcus' death. Nearly 12% of these foster parents had criminal histories, including charges such as child endangerment, domestic violence, and DUI (Coolidge, 2007).

Think about what this means for children who have been beaten, starved, or left alone in dirty cribs. Think about what this means for children who have never been hugged and kissed, read a bedtime story, or had pajamas. Think of the children who have seen their parents shoot heroin so often they can imitate it with precision, yet they can't count to ten. These are the children who rely on foster parents to show them a better world and a better life.

My husband and I have three children. If today we were unable to take care of them and did not have any extended family or friends willing to step up and raise them, they would be placed in foster care. In Hamilton County, they would have more than a one in ten chance of moving into homes with adults who had engaged in criminal activity. They would lose their school, their friends, and probably each other. Why is this OK with the rest of us?

It's not OK, which was evidenced by the sheer volume of people who were outraged when they began learning about such statistics. Unfortunately, during this time, Marcus' community members were not often encouraged to become part of the solution. Returning to the analogy of a football game, it was as if chaos was erupting on the field while the referees told the crowd they had it all under control.

While there is certainly a place for policies and procedures regarding foster care placement, such policies and procedures tend to be black and white answers to problems where endless shades of gray exist. For example, one foster parent was found to have a fifteen-year-old criminal history relating to the possession of drugs. He was twenty-five at the time of the charge. He had hit rock bottom then, but had recovered from his addictions. At the time his history was revealed, he had been clean for fourteen years. He was a counselor at a drug-rehabilitation center and worked with at-risk youth. He became a foster parent for two teenage brothers. The boys had been spiraling out of control with delinquent behavior. With the guidance, support, and role modeling of this foster father, both boys began turning their lives around. They were attending school daily and involved in numerous extra-curricular activities. Although this man had been recognized for his positive impact and the message he brought to his community, he was at risk of having his foster care license revoked.

On the other hand, another foster parenting couple was caring for three young foster children under the age of five. These foster parents had three biological children and had adopted four others, for a total of ten children. The toddlers were regularly left in the care of the older children and sustained multiple physical injuries as a result of a lack of supervision. They missed crucial medical appointments and were behind on immunizations. There were prior concerns noted regarding other foster children in their home, including educational neglect. However, the foster parents did not have any criminal history, and despite concerns raised to the Children's Services agency, they continued fostering.

During the immediate aftermath of Marcus' death, Senator Tom Niehaus was quietly working behind the scenes to learn about the issues facing foster children and how they could be better protected. Several months after Marcus' death, he brought together a group of lawmakers, child advo-cates, foster and adoptive parents, and former foster children who were now adults. As a result of the work done by this group and other senators, several new house and senate bills were created and eventually signed into law by Governor Ted Strickland.

Perhaps the most important of these changes made in Ohio law following Marcus' death involves a statewide fingerprint database designed to alert public children's services agencies if a foster parent was arrested. Prior to Senate Bill 163, there was no mechanism in place to facilitate this kind of communication between law enforcement officials and children's services agencies. If Senate Bill 163 had been created prior to Marcus' death, Butler County Children's Services would have been notified immediately when David Carroll was arrested for domestic violence against his wife in June 2006. Upon such notification, Marcus, along with any other foster children, would have been removed from the Carrolls' home. Such a law could have saved Marcus' life.

Other changes in state law included increasing the hours of training for foster parents from twenty-four to thirty-six. This change was introduced in hope that foster parents would be better equipped to understand the needs of foster children and better handle their care. Additionally, experienced foster parents would be encouraged to mentor other foster parents and provide ongoing support.

These are good steps to take in tightening the reigns on foster care. However, training, mentoring, and oversight of foster parents cannot guarantee that children will be safe. Although dozens of laws exist to protect and help children like Adam and Sarah, the law does not require foster parents to love and nurture their foster children. Laws cannot make foster parents begin and end each day rocking a child into their first sense of comfort and predictability. Laws cannot ensure that a child will be loved. At the end of the day, they cannot wrap their arms around children the way Adam's foster mom held Sarah to her chest while she sobbed. At best, laws are band-aids on a gaping wound.

As the media coverage of foster care continued, it rarely shed a positive light on foster parents. Being a good, quality foster parent is a tough job on any given day. Fostering children during the time following Marcus' death was especially challenging.

Nana and Pop were sick over Marcus' death and desperately wanted better care for all foster children. During a time in which they should have been praised and appreciated for their loving care, they felt degraded.

About a month after Marcus died, Nana ran an errand to the grocery store with Adam and Sarah in tow. While waiting in line for the cashier, the foster mom overheard a verbal exchange between the cashier and the customer in front of her. The two were lamenting the state of foster care, each further convincing the other that foster parents were only in it for the money. Nana attempted to divert Adam and Sarah's attention from the animated discussion. She silently prayed the children wouldn't hear the conversation about foster care. Just when she thought it was over, the customer made a parting comment. "If I had to choose between foster care and death for my child, I would choose death."

It didn't matter that the comment was made out of ignorance or mean-ness. All that mattered was it pierced Nana's heart and brought tears to her eyes, while Adam and Sarah simply looked at each other.

Adam and Sarah were quiet as Nana held Adam's hand and pushed the cart holding Sarah out to the car. Sarah happily played with a doll in the backseat on the ride home, oblivious to what had transpired at the store. Adam, however, had questions.

"I'm a foster kid, right, Nana?"

"Adam, you are a wonderful six-year-old who is loving and kind and very smart. And yes, you happen to be in foster care."

"Those ladies weren't saying nice things, were they?"

"No Adam, but sometimes when people don't understand something they talk nonsense."

Adam seemed to accept this, and for him, the moment had passed, but Nana's heart remained heavy. She was not alone in carrying the added burden of being suspect and degraded during this time. Many foster parents reported feeling looked down upon and judged negatively because of their choice to foster. This kind of negativity against foster parents seemed to play out in the numbers of people who sought more information on becoming foster parents. Hamilton County Children's Services reported that twenty-nine people inquired about becoming foster parents in August 2006, and that following the incident with Marcus Fiesel and the ongoing press coverage, in December, just four months later, only two people inquired (Zimmerman, 2007). Hamilton County Children's Services had difficulty recruiting new foster parents amidst the negative publicity the agency was receiving. Some foster families quit fostering, and a number of other foster homes were closed due to revelations in the foster parent's criminal histories.

Although the number of foster homes decreased, the number of children needing foster care placement did not. When this happens, children are often placed in foster homes much further away from everything that they've come to know.

Imagine being a child who has been violated by your parents, the people who are supposed to take care of you. Imagine getting into a stranger's car and having no control over where it is going. You round the corner where you used to wait for the bus with your mother, and you keep going. You pass the grocery store you recognize, the buildings you've seen before fly by. Familiar landmarks vanish and time passes. In time, you are in completely foreign territory. And, you are being left there. Everything you know is hours away.

Infants and toddlers placed at a distance must endure long car rides each week. A caseworker or case aide might have to travel two hours to pick them up for weekly visits with their parents and then have a two-hour drive for the return trip. The children arrive tired and cranky. Surely, this impacts the quality of the family visit. They visit for two hours with their mom or dad, and then are driven back to their foster homes. It is heartbreaking when, too often, a parent fails to show.

A case aide or caseworker in this scenario spends the entire day traveling. If a case-aide is not available to transport, the responsibility falls to the caseworker. When that happens, the caseworker is taken from other critical duties, such as home visits with other at-risk children. From a purely financial standpoint, think about the cost of gas and the salaries involved.

Another downside to children being placed far away is the reality that it is harder to monitor how a placement is going. Caseworkers or GALs sometimes conduct unannounced visits at foster homes. It is too much of a gamble to drive two hours and find that there is no one home. Foster home visits may not be conducted as frequently when distance to the placement is a factor.

Finally, a caseworker or GAL is less likely to have a working knowledge of the services available to help children in unfamiliar towns. While I have a good understanding of area service providers, I most likely won't know anything about, or have any firsthand experience with, service providers located far away.

The current lack of local foster homes in Hamilton County for children is a significant problem that did not exist five years ago. It adds a new layer of difficulty to helping children who are in crisis. Sometimes when I am with my own kids, at their schools or sports activities, I look around at all of the families and wonder why, with so many good families and committed parents, is it so hard to find a home for children? What would help these people decide to commit to fostering or adopting?

The effects of Marcus' case played out in the media for months following his death. The media sought court orders to open the records of foster parents, reasoning that children would be better protected in foster care if there were less secrecy surrounding foster care placements and licensed foster parents. I thought of little Michelle, of a two-year-old foster girl who suffered from chronic, sexually transmitted diseases, courtesy of her father. Her location was carefully hidden due to her parent's threats to kill the people taking care of her. How would opening foster parents' records protect her?

While politicians, newspaper reporters, and child welfare professionals battled in the fallout of Marcus' case, Nana and Pop quietly went about the business of sheltering Adam and Sarah from ugly truths that permeated every fabric of life in Marcus' community. Although they were worried about how this would affect Adam and Sarah's placement in their home, they were careful not to let on any signs of stress or worry. When caseworkers made their home visits and talked about Marcus' case and how it would affect all children placed in Lifeway foster homes, they were redirected and asked not to discuss it within earshot of the children.

By now, Adam and Sarah were firmly rooted in their foster family and growing by leaps and bounds. They were experiencing childhood magic in the form of two loving caregivers, exposure to letters and numbers that were beginning to make sense, freedom to explore nature, the chance to make real and imaginary friends. For the first time, their world was stable, filled with order and routine along with healthy doses of nurturing and love.

Returning to the football analogy, the game of Adam and Sarah was going well. They were together and safe, loved and nurtured. The chaos from Marcus' game threatened to spill over into theirs. If all children placed in Lifeway foster homes were removed, Adam would be ripped from the arms of the foster mother who rocked him at the beginning and end of each day. Sarah would be ripped from the arms of the foster mother who held her to her chest while she sobbed on the night of her arrival in her home. Quite possibly, Adam and Sarah would be ripped from each other once again.

CHAPTER 7

Finding a Forever Family

L IFE CONTINUED AS USUAL for Adam and Sarah, while chaos enveloped the foster care system responsible for ensuring their needs. They didn't know there was a possibility of being removed from the home and people they had grown to love. Nana and Pop, however, feared the children would be uprooted again as rumors spread of Lifeway for Youth's closing. They held their breaths each time the doorbell rang. Would a caseworker come and take Adam and Sarah away?

Shortly after Marcus' death, the trial to terminate Adam and Sarah's parents' rights was completed. When the big day of trial finally arrived, Lisa testified about the parents' history and their criminal behavior. She answered many questions about the history of the case and what had led to Adam and Sarah's placement in foster care. She testified that neither parent would be available to care for them within the foreseeable future, and that there were no relatives willing or able to care for the children.

The magistrate took three months to render her decision. Sometimes these decisions are made in a timely manner. Sometimes they drag on for what seems an eternity. There are a number of reasons for this from paperwork delays to overloaded dockets. The ruling of termination of parental rights is likened to a death sentence for a family. In the eyes of the law, biological parents are reduced to strangers to their children. They can never come back to retrieve them, even if they substantially improve their lives and parenting capabilities.

Once the magistrate ruled that termination of parental rights was in Adam and Sarah's best interests, their caseworker transferred the case to a new social worker from the Adoptions Unit at Children's Services. Their present foster parents felt they were too old to raise them permanently, though they were willing to act as unofficial grandparents to Adam and Sarah for the rest of their lives. After all, they would be in their late seventies when Adam and Sarah became teenagers. Since they were not planning to adopt, the new caseworker was responsible for finding an adoptive home for them.

By this time Adam was seven years old and Sarah was five. The chances of finding adoptive families decrease as children age. Luckily, Adam and Sarah were still young enough to have a good chance at being adopted. The new caseworker began reading over home studies. Home studies tell the story of potential adoptive families. These are families that have completed training and have been licensed to adopt. Their home studies include information such as their family composition, what kinds of kids they are open to adopting, their financial and medical histories, and their career information. Photos of the potential adoptive family are included in addition to a description of their hobbies and what they like to do. Pictures of Adam and Sarah were placed on a state-run Web site so that potential adoptive families from around the country could inquire about the children.

The caseworker sifted through available families and narrowed the choices down to five prospects. A meeting of the Matching and Selection

Committee was held to decide which family would be offered the chance to adopt Adam and Sarah. This meeting is held weekly at Children's Services. Members of this committee include the child's adoption caseworker, the GAL and/or Court Appointed Special Advocate, an adoption supervisor, a caseworker for each family being considered for a child, and a community representative. Other people are present as well, such as the coordinator for the weekly meetings as well as a clerical support person. A child's therapist may be invited to impart information or recommendations. He or she is then excused.

At the meeting, caseworkers present children who need an adoptive home and match them with adoptive families. The caseworker tells the story of the child and provides any information available about birth history, medical history, previous foster placements, behavior problems, and special needs or any other information that will help the committee members get a sense of the child.

After a child is presented, potential adoptive families are presented. There may be ten families to present for one child, and only two for another child, depending on the child and his or her needs or behavioral problems. There may be a number of families seeking an infant, but only one or two willing to adopt older children.

Once all of the families are presented, the committee members vote on which family would be best for which child. The family with the most votes is officially matched with the child, and visits occur with the intention of the child's adoption by this family.

As a Guardian Ad Litem, I have attended many such meetings. Each time I leave, I feel unsettled about the way the system "makes" families. Every time I vote for a family, I feel insignificantly small and burdened. Who am I to decide a child's future? Who am I to have a hand in casting their fate?

Then I realize that I am one of the few people sitting around the table who have ever actually met the child.

Adam and Sarah were presented at Matching and Selection Committee at 10 a.m. on a Thursday morning. Other children, also available for adoption, were presented in other timeslots that day.

Adam's caseworker began her presentation of Adam and Sarah by briefly describing the reason the children were removed from their parents and how long they had been in foster care. She talked about Adam's history of behavior problems and the progress he had made in his foster home and in therapy. She reported that Adam was bright and doing well in first grade. Although he occasionally got into trouble at school, he did well academically and got along well, for the most part, with other children.

Likewise, she described Sarah as developmentally on target and doing well in the foster home. She had made a good adjustment to Adam's foster home and did not have any behavior problems that were not typical for a five-year-old. Sarah loved baby dolls and coloring books. At times, she was stubborn and angry, but could be redirected fairly easily.

The caseworker went on to describe details about the children and how they spend their time in their foster home. She talked about how the children loved nature and spent lots of time roaming the outdoors with their foster parents. She had pictures of Adam and Sarah taken during the fall, both of them leaning against a giant oak tree with beautiful orange leaves against a blue sky.

After Adam and Sarah were presented, the five potential families identified by the caseworker were presented. The five families identified for Adam and Sarah were as follows:

Mr. and Mrs. Ted Smith: Ted and Helen Smith had two teenage girls, ages twelve and fourteen. They wanted to adopt up to three children under the age of eight. Both Ted and Helen came from big families and had a strong extended family support system. Helen worked full time as an administrative assistant in a large corporation and Ted worked full time as a computer technician. Neither had any medical problems. Their current income was stable; however, they had filed bankruptcy three years earlier. The father was a recovering alcoholic and had been sober for two years. They lived an hour south of Adam and Sarah's foster parents and were willing to continue a relationship with them.

Mr. and Mrs. William Jones: Bill and Mary Jones did not have any children due to infertility issues. They were interested in adopting up to two siblings under the age of six. Bill was a chemical engineer and Mary worked in retail. They planned for Mary to quit her job when they adopted. They had moved to town a year ago after a job transfer, and would likely move every few years due to Bill's job. Mary was currently on medication and being treated by a therapist for depression. Bill and Mary had friends in the area. They did not have an extended family support system locally, and they had not decided whether they were willing to continue relationships with former foster parents.

Ms. Michelle Walker: Michelle was a kindergarten teacher and had never been married. When she was fourteen, her parents adopted four boys ranging in age from fourteen to five. They successfully raised all four, despite the emotional problems these children had. Michelle's parents were supportive of her decision to adopt and would help her as needed. Her income was sufficient and her medical history revealed no concerns regarding her health. She lived in the same town as Adam and Sarah and was open to ongoing contact with their foster parents.

Mr. and Mrs. Keith Wagner: Keith and Kelly had three children ages five, six, and eight. They had adopted all three children. They lived in West

Virginia on a farm, and Keith was the pastor of a small, rural church. Their children were home-schooled by Kelly and Keith worked nearby and came home for lunch every day. They had experienced some financial difficulties in the past, but were currently making ends meet. They were experienced adoptive parents, and believed their children made better adjustments to their home when contact between former foster parents ceased.

Ms. Caroline Davis: Ms. Davis was a single woman with two grown children. She was a retired schoolteacher. Her children were twenty-four and twenty-six. They both lived nearby and had good relationships with their mother. She lived two hours north of Adam and Sarah's current placement. Caroline was a breast cancer survivor. Her doctor had written a letter in support of her intention to adopt. She was willing to continue a relationship with Adam and Sarah's foster parents.

After each family was presented, the people around the table asked questions. Sometimes there were few questions of the caseworkers presenting potential families. Other times the question and answer session was lengthy. When all the questions had been answered, each member at the table cast a vote for the family he or she thought would be the best match. The family that got the most votes, got the children.

If you were attending a Matching and Selection Committee meeting, which family would you choose? Imagine what the presentation of Adam and Sarah would look like had things gone differently. Suppose Adam had never arrived at the front door of the foster parents he had grown to love. Suppose he went to foster parents who didn't have the time, desire, or dedication it took to help him heal. Suppose he was placed in the home of Liz and David Carroll. All too easily, the caseworker's presentation of Adam and Sarah could have sounded like this: Adam, Caucasian male, age seven. Adam was removed from his biological parents at age four due to the parents' criminal activity and significant family violence. He is currently in first grade and receiving special education services due to speech delays, cognitive delays, and behavioral problems. He has been diagnosed with Reactive Attachment Disorder, Post Traumatic Stress Disorder, and Attention Deficit Disorder. He is currently on three different psychotropic medications to help with impulse control and hyperactivity. He has lived in seven different foster homes since his initial removal from his parents. His behavior problems include aggression and bed-wetting.

Sarah, Caucasian female, age five. Sarah is Adam's younger sibling. They were separated shortly after their initial placement in foster care and have not seen each other since, due to Adam's aggression toward her. Caseworker is not recommending adoptive placement in the same home as Adam. Sarah is speech delayed and has coordination issues. She receives speech therapy and physical therapy to help further develop her motor skills. She is quiet and withdrawn but when she smiles, she lights up the room. One set of previous foster parents had been interested in adopting her, but they divorced and neither was able to care for Sarah after that time. She is currently living in her third foster home. Her foster parents do not wish to adopt her.

Without the joint efforts of Nana, Pop, and Mary, the therapist, Adam's progress would likely not have occurred. Chances are his behavior problems likely would have escalated and continued to spiral out of control. He would have gotten two years bigger and two years stronger, and more and more difficult to help. Many potential families may have backed away, fearing their ability to handle him.

Adam and Sarah are lucky because there are families interested in adopting them. Some children, particularly older children, wait for a forever home without one on the horizon. In Hamilton County, there are, at any given time, about two hundred children waiting to be adopted. These are the children who do not belong to a family. Too many never will.

Each month a list crosses my desk at work. This list is the agenda for the Matching and Selection Committee meeting. I look it over to see whether I am the Guardian Ad Litem for any children being presented. After I scan the list for familiar names, my eyes fall on the names of countless others. Next to many of them, a box is checked: child presentation only, no families to present. These are the children who are languishing in foster care waiting for a forever family, for a place to belong and to call their own. While they wait, they live in foster homes with foster parents who do not wish to adopt them. Many of them have moved from home to home without ever experiencing stability. The older they get, the less likely a family will come forward to love them.

A recent study conducted by the US Census Bureau found that millions of Americans have considered fostering or adopting children (U.S. Census Bureau, 2006). Unfortunately, very few of these people follow through. There are many misconceptions regarding children in foster care, particularly infants and young children. Because infants and toddlers are the fastest growing segment of children in foster care, it is essential to educate communities about the foster care and adoption processes.

I'm always surprised when I hear people say they did not know they could adopt a baby in America without having the chance of a biological parent returning to get the infant. When parents' rights are terminated, they lose all legal rights to their children. Under these circumstances, biological parents are never able to seek a return of custody.

Furthermore, in Hamilton County there is a shortage of foster homes for babies and young children. A good number of these young children become available for adoption after efforts to reunify them with their parents fail. For example, let's say a mother and father have three children and the kids are placed in foster care while the parents undergo services such as drug treatment or mental health treatment. The parents fail consistently and repeatedly to do what is required by the court to have their children safely returned to them. A termination of parental rights trial is conducted, and the magistrate decides it is in the children's best interests for them to be adopted. Let's assume the three children are adopted together and live happily ever after.

Months, or even several years later, mom and dad have a new baby. They have never successfully completed services and they still have drug problems or mental health problems. When this happens, the baby is placed in foster care from the hospital and the Children's Services agency can file for termination of parental rights without having to offer the parents services all over again. The parents have already demonstrated an inability to care for their older children. Unless they show they have considerably altered their lives, there is a good chance their baby will be permanently committed and made available for adoption.

Across America, there are an estimated 114,000 children eligible and waiting to be adopted (Foster Care Adoption Fact Sheet). There are hundreds, if not thousands, of children waiting for adoption who entered the system as young as Adam and Sarah. For their best interests, the court severed their parents' rights. They will never be permitted to return to their biological parents. The problem is they end up in a holding pattern without a new family to embrace them. For reasons beyond their control, they are left to languish in the system, moving from home to home with a meager bag of belongings, while the baggage they carry in their hearts and souls grows exponentially.

I wonder what it is like to be a child who lives in this holding pattern. Let's suppose you are nine years old and living in a world where things are not good. You awake in the morning on a filthy mattress next to your six-year-old brother. Your stomach growls with hunger and you shiver in the cold winter air. The heat has been turned off in the apartment because the electricity bill was not paid. Your mom is passed out on the couch, drug paraphernalia lying next to her bone-thin body. You get yourself and your little brother dressed and off to school.

You try not to double over in pain as you walk, desperate to conceal the swollen abdomen that was kicked last night by your mom's boyfriend. But it's no use. The school nurse calls you to the office. Your game is up. The words begin to roll off your tongue as you describe the drugs and the convicted felon who is selling them out of your apartment. You speak of the violence between your mom and her felon boyfriend and the hunger in the pit of your stomach that will not go away. You are scared to go home and for the first time you admit that to people who can help you. A caseworker appears, and you and your brother will not be going home tonight. You will stay with a foster family while your mom gets herself together.

But your mom doesn't get herself together. Weeks, months, and years pass. Adults decide you and your little brother will never go home. You will be adopted. The door on your old life will be closed forever. There is no going back. Your mother is no longer your mother in the eyes of the law. But there is no one who wants to take her place. So you and your little brother wait. And wait. And wait. You change foster homes several times because they just aren't working out. You wake up and you are a teenager. You wait some more. On your eighteenth birthday, you are told you are free to go, to be on your own and take care of yourself. You step into a world which you have no idea how to navigate. You look for your mom. You cannot find her. There is no one to take her place.

Behind each of the 114,000 children waiting to be adopted, there lies a story like this one. The stories are as unique as facial features, but hauntingly similar. Each one of these precious children was born into a life that failed to give them the foundation they desperately needed: a place to call their own, with people who love them. Forever.

The average child waits for an adoptive family for more than three years. Over 20% will wait five years or more (Foster Care Adoption Fact Sheet). Kids have a hard time waiting. Waiting for their turn at bat. Waiting for their birthdays. For summer vacation. Imagine how many kids are waiting… for families.

Adam and Sarah did not have to wait long for a forever family to call their own. The Matching and Selection Committee debated for nearly two hours before each of the nine members cast a secret vote for a family. The Jones family and Caroline Davis received one vote. The Smith and Wagner families each received two votes. Michelle Walker, the kindergarten teacher, received three votes. On that Thursday at the Matching and Selection Committee meeting, Adam and Sarah were matched with Ms. Walker. A family was made.

It is important to note that if the Guardian Ad Litem objects to a match, he or she can file a motion in court and ask the magistrate not to approve the match or the placement with the family selected. Trial would then be conducted and the magistrate may rule that the parties go back to the pool of potential families and select another one. For example, the committee may match a child with a family that lives far away, despite the therapist's recommendation that the child stay local if possible in order to maintain the therapeutic relationship. If there are local families available, the GAL may object. If Children's Services plans to move forward with placement anyway, the GAL can seek court intervention to stop the move.

Ms. Michelle Walker was notified that she was matched with a little boy and a little girl named Adam and Sarah. She could have accepted the match or not, after hearing about them. She didn't hesitate when asked. Many months later Ms. Walker's mother told the caseworker that when Michelle was little and played with her dolls she considered them her adopted children. She had always wanted to grow a family this way.

Adam's therapist began preparing him for the move to an adoptive home. Sarah joined in some of these sessions as well. Both of them were apprehensive and did not want to leave their foster parents. Following the therapist's recommendations, the foster parents also began talking to the children about Michelle. Pictures of Michelle and her extended family were sent to Adam's therapist, and together she, Adam, and Sarah talked about the people in the pictures and how they had always hoped a little boy and a little girl would come into their lives.

Nana and Pop were open to meeting Michelle and spending time with her. Likewise, Michelle was anxious to meet not only Adam and Sarah, but also the people who had loved and cared for them so well. One spring morning, after preparation by the therapist, Nana and Pop, along with Adam and Sarah, drove to a park a few miles from their home. The kids were quiet in the backseat. They knew they were going to meet Michelle for the first time. Old feelings of dread coursed through their veins. They did not know what to expect. All they wanted was the familiarity of the foster parents they had come to count on.

When they arrived at the park, Adam and Sarah refused to get out of the car. They just sat there. Anticipating this reaction, Nana and Pop promised them that this was only a visit, and they would be with them the whole time. Afterward, as previously planned, they would go to the children's favorite pizza place. Having planned the rest of the day in advance seemed to comfort Adam and Sarah, and they reluctantly climbed out of the car.

This first meeting was anticlimactic. There were no instantaneous hugs, no love at first sight, or riding off into the sunset. Adam and Sarah did not have much to do with Michelle. They went to Nana and Pop for help with shoestrings and pushes on swings. Michelle wasn't worried. She enjoyed watching them play and understood that it would take time before the children grew comfortable with her. After all, she was a stranger. They spent a couple of hours at the park and then went their separate ways.

Later, as Nan, Pop, Adam, and Sarah shared a pepperoni pizza, they talked about their trip to the park and meeting Michelle. Adam and Sarah didn't have much to say about their day. They thought Michelle seemed nice and agreed that they would like to visit with her again.

During the next week, Michelle and Nana talked on the phone several times. They got along well and enjoyed talking about the children. Michelle had a million questions and Nana liked that Michelle wanted to know so much. A friendship between them grew naturally.

The next weekend, the five of them met again, this time at McDonald's. Michelle and the children were planning to spend the day together. After lunch, they said good-bye to Nana and Pop and went to visit Michelle's house. They played there for the afternoon, had a dinner of spaghetti and meatballs, and then returned to their foster home. Nana and Pop were waiting when they returned. The children both ran up the front steps and through the door, happy from their day out, but happy to be home as well. They hugged Michelle good-bye and waved to her from the living room window as her car backed out of the driveway.

Adam's weekly therapy sessions continued, during which time he talked about his old mom, Nana, and Michelle, who would be his new mom. He played board games with his therapist while she gently helped him explore his feelings and make sense of the changes that were occurring. By now, the therapist and Adam had many conversations about "the mommy job" and how some mommies, even though they loved their kids, weren't able to do the job it took to take care of them. They had talked about how Nana and Pop had done the mommy job and daddy job when Adam's mommy and daddy could not do it. But Adam needed someone to do the mommy job forever, and Michelle very much wanted to do the mommy job for both Adam and his sister.

Over the next month Michelle's visits with Adam and Sarah continued, culminating in weekend visits during which they spent the night. Adam's therapist arranged for a meeting in her office with Nana and Pop, Michelle and Adam and Sarah. Together the adults talked to Adam and Sarah about living with Michelle forever. They planned to move at the beginning of the summer, so that Michelle would have the whole summer to spend with them and help them adjust to their new life together before school began and she returned to work.

The big day arrived and Adam and Sarah moved into Michelle's house. They had been leaving some of their belongings there ever since their first sleepover, and were happy to be surrounded by familiar things. Nana and Pop were sad to see them go, but devoted to helping them make a good adjustment to their new home. Nana had made Adam and Sarah each special quilts to take with them, "sown with love and kisses," she told them as they unwrapped their packages. Knowing they could call and visit helped Adam and Sarah face the next chapter in their lives.

Adam's therapist continued seeing him during this time, and helped him sort through his feelings. Sometimes Sarah joined in these sessions. Michelle attended each week as well and relied on the therapist for support and suggestions in helping the family settle into a routine and build their relationships with one another.

Michelle's parents proved to be an invaluable support to all of them as they melded into a family unit. Likewise, Michelle's adopted brothers took a special interest in Adam and Sarah and spent hours with them swimming and playing ball outside.

The summer months drew to a close, and Adam and Sarah began school where their adoptive mother taught kindergarten. Adam began second grade without a major incident, although he found himself in trouble at least once a week, mostly testing limits. When his teacher told him not to talk in the hallway, he continued to chatter away. On occasion, he would snatch a classroom item out of another child's hands. Lunchroom monitors constantly had to remind him to quiet down and finish his lunch. He rarely would listen, and spent part of his recess sitting in time out while the other children played. Michelle handled each behavior problem as it occurred and worked with her colleagues to help Adam make better choices. Sarah was placed in a kindergarten classroom different from her mother, and experienced ups and downs as well. Once she showed her underwear to a group of girls on the playground. Another time she took a library book without asking and didn't say a word while the teacher asked the children whether anyone had seen it. Nevertheless, they made steady progress and appeared to be genuinely happy.

Eight months after Adam and Sarah went to live with Michelle, their adoption was finalized in court. Michelle sat at a small wooden table facing the judge's bench, with Adam on her left and Sarah on her right. Michelle's parents and brothers, the adoption caseworker, Nana and Pop, and Adam's therapist packed the courtroom. When the judge asked Michelle why she wanted to adopt Adam and Sarah, she paused before responding. "I saw the way my parents devoted themselves to raising me and my four adopted brothers. I always knew there would be no better way to spend my life than to share my life and my love with children who needed me."

The judge turned his attention to Adam and Sarah. "Adam, do you want to be adopted by Michelle Walker?" Adam looked at him and fidgeted in his seat. He slowly nodded his head. When the judge asked him why, he held Michelle's hand and whispered, "Because she is my forever mommy."

The judge smiled and leaned over just a bit, looking at Sarah. "What do think about this, Sarah?"

Sarah looked up at him and didn't hesitate before declaring in her big, six-year-old voice, "I love her!"

Four years have passed since Adam and Sarah's adoption. They are happy, healthy, and growing every day. The past four years have not been without adjustment problems and setbacks. There was the time Adam got mad at a classmate and kicked him in the head. And the time Sarah mysteriously began wetting the bed every night at age seven. Many times Michelle called her parents crying and overwhelmed, worried about Adam's sudden bursts of anger or Sarah's complete defiance that appeared out of nowhere.

Luckily, Michelle, Adam, and Sarah have an army of support behind them in the form of their extended family and Nana and Pop. From time to time, they also make visits to therapy when they need a little extra help. Because Adam and Sarah are adopted, Michelle receives a monthly subsidy for both of the children and is able to save for their college tuition. All of these supports strengthen the family and help secure their futures.

Adam and Sarah did not ride off into the sunset, but day-by-day, they are making it. They face their future together when they could have easily been separated forever. They are firmly rooted in a family and community that are committed to them, instead of drifting from home to home without a sense of family. They know who they are and who loves them. They know where they have come from and where they can go. A foster care system, loving foster parents, a compassionate therapist, and a single woman who said yes gave them a chance at a childhood. And, a chance at a future.

CHAPTER 8

Helping Hands

DIAMOND WAS NINE YEARS old when I first met her. She was a beautiful little girl with big, green eyes and dark wavy hair. She was built like a runner, graceful and fluid. Her shy smile melted my heart. The depth revealed in her green eyes seemed well beyond nine years.

I was a Children's Services caseworker at the time, fresh out of college and on my first real job for only two months when I met her. Diamond's case was among the first I received. When I was assigned to her case, I absorbed myself in all four volumes of the family case file. It read like a horror story.

Diamond was two years old when her father was found shot dead outside a bar. At that time, she lived with their mother in a filthy apartment. Roaches roamed the floors and walls and dirty dishes overflowed in the kitchen sink. Wheelchair bound, Diamond's mother did the best she could to raise her, a task made nearly impossible by her diagnoses of muscular dystrophy and AIDS.

Diamond was three years old when she and her mother moved in with her mother's older cousin, Beverly. Beverly promised to take care of the family. Diamond was seven years old when her mother died. She continued living with Beverly, whom she referred to as her aunt.

Diamond's mother had been dead for just a couple of years when I first met the family. A nineteen-year-old neighbor had sexually abused Diamond. Her testimony at his trial resulted in a rape conviction and sentencing of five years in prison. Despite the trauma of assault and testifying at the trial, Beverly refused to seek therapy for the little girl. My job was to monitor Diamond's case and ensure she received therapy to deal with the issues of sexual abuse. Beverly did not drive and would not take her to therapy.

Since the case was open simply to ensure Diamond received therapy, I assumed my task was simply to make sure she got there. Each week, I dutifully took Diamond to see her therapist, a young woman who was working as a therapy intern while she went to graduate school to obtain her master's degree in counseling. I would retrieve Diamond from her home and drive her to therapy. I did paperwork while I waited during her fifty-minute session. At the end of each session, the therapist and I would touch base about how things were going. Then I would drive Diamond home. As much as I encouraged Beverly to become involved in her therapy, she refused. Beverly struck me as a stern woman, but I didn't have any reason to believe she wasn't taking care of Diamond. She was getting to school, had food on the table and a roof over her head. It was enough.

I enjoyed spending some time with Diamond and getting to know her. She was lively and pleasant and seemed to enjoy the time in the car. One day while I was driving her home, I told her that I would miss our appointment the next week, but that another driver would take her to therapy. She pressed for the reason why and I told her that I was getting married and that I would be on vacation the following week.

She asked, "Can I come to the wedding?"

I jokingly asked why she would want to come. Her face lit up and she clasped her hands together and in all her nine-year-old wonder said, "So I can kiss the bride, of course." She was full of dreams and possibilities. The innocence of that moment was so pure. For a split second, I wanted to invite her and Beverly, but I knew that would cross a professional line. So, I simply smiled and kept driving.

In time, two-dozen more families were added to my caseload. As hard as I tried to find time in my schedule, it was impossible to continue devoting two hours each week to Diamond and her therapy appointments. Besides, her therapist reported that she wasn't making much progress in dealing with the abuse she had endured. In the meantime, I became so overwhelmed with my daily job responsibilities that I lost sight of Diamond as a child who had grown fond of me and relished our weekly drive to and from sessions. I saw her as a case that could be handled by a case aide, a co-worker whose job was to simply transport children from one place to another. I'm sure I must have told Diamond and Beverly that another person would begin transporting her to and from therapy, but I don't remember doing so. And then, I moved on to the next family in crisis.

A handful of these two-dozen families could not make the changes needed to live any differently than they had been, and I was faced with the horrible task of removing children from abusive and neglectful parents. It was at this time that I became familiar with an agency called ProKids. From the moment I met Charlotte, a Guardian Ad Litem from ProKids, I knew that someday I wanted to work at ProKids with her. She respectfully, and passionately, advocated on behalf of children. I watched her address the court on matters pertaining to a child and I felt like I caught my first glimpse of common sense and compassion in a world full of madness. I was at court observing a veteran caseworker who was discussing a thirteen-year-old boy named Aaron. Aaron was living in foster care but desperately wanted to live with his twenty-five-year-old uncle. The caseworker was adamantly opposed to the idea, stating his uncle was too young to raise a teenage boy. Charlotte felt like it was important to explore, if only to honor Aaron's request and show him that the team was listening to him. It may not be in his best interest, she stated, but it was definitely not in his best interest to rule it out immediately without any investigation. I began researching ProKids and its mission of ensuring a safe, permanent, and nurturing home for every child. What I learned was fascinating.

Long before Marcus Fiesel was born, a need for intensive advocacy for abused and neglected children was noted. In 1977, Judge David Soukup from Seattle, Washington developed a plan to train and supervise community volunteer advocates. These advocates would learn as much as possible about these children and come into his courtroom to tell him about their needs. Under his leadership, the National Court Appointed Special Advocate Association was born. Court Appointed Special Advocates (CASAs) are assigned to children who have been abused and neglected, and are responsible for monitoring every aspect of their case.

Operating in Cincinnati, Ohio for over twenty-five years, ProKids' CASA Program has been training and supervising community volunteers. Armed with very detailed information about a child, CASAs make recommendations to juvenile court magistrates regarding their best interests. CASAs work diligently on behalf of children to ensure they receive everything they need while they belong to a government system as opposed to a loving family.

The process to become a CASA is in some ways more intensive than the process to become a foster parent. ProKids staff conducts a formal interview with each candidate. Candidates complete 30 hours of classroom instruction, undergo thorough background checks, provide references, and observe a court hearing. They are assigned to a case only after all requirements are satisfied. Because they are assigned to only one or two families at a time, they are able to devote significant attention to a case when many other professionals simply cannot.

It is important to note that counties and states differ in how the role of the CASA is practiced. In Cincinnati, Ohio, CASAs are appointed to cases in tandem with a ProKids Staff GAL. The GAL offers guidance and support to a CASA and assists them in navigating the system on behalf of children. In return, the CASA offers hands that hold critical details of these children's lives that may otherwise be overlooked. Together, the ProKids CASA and GAL make a powerful team. They attend each court hearing to report their findings and recommendations. They may agree or disagree with other parties to the case, such as the Children's Services caseworker or biological parents. When disagreements occur, trial is held and the magistrate issues a ruling or court order pertaining to the case.

As a Children's Services worker, I knew that the system could only do so much. When I worked with a ProKids GAL and CASA, I felt like I had allies in my struggles to help children. The work was easier to bear when I had other people who were committed to children and able to help them get what they needed. When I wasn't sure whether a child could safely return home, the ProKids GAL and CASA were there to investigate the possibility as well and offer an opinion. Oftentimes, there were things I could not request in court due to budget restraints, such as tutoring. The GAL and CASA from ProKids would diligently set about finding a free tutoring program and help make the arrangements for a child to participate. Working together lifted a burden from me. I began to see that there could be happy endings to painful life stories.

When ProKids had a job opening for a Guardian Ad Litem, I didn't hesitate to apply. I believed in ProKids' mission and had seen firsthand how volunteers improved the lives of children languishing in the system. I wanted to be a part of that. After four years, I left Children's Services to join a team I had always admired.

After I joined ProKids in 1998, I often wondered what had happened to many of the children I had met as a caseworker. Nine-year-old Diamond crossed my mind more than most. By now, she would have been fourteen, and into her teenage years. How was she doing?

Within days, I had my answer in the form of a new case that had come into the ProKids office. Diamond had been placed in foster care a week before. Beverly had refused to continue caring for her. She was alleged to have substance abuse problems. Diamond needed a Guardian Ad Litem to represent her. I offered to take this new case. I wanted a second chance to help the little girl who wanted to kiss the bride. My first task was to assign a volunteer to act as Diamond's CASA. Kelly was a logical choice.

Kelly was a married mother of nine children. Her youngest had entered kindergarten and she was ready to spend some time helping children who didn't have the luxury of a happy home life. Kelly understood children, and knew how to nurture them, better than anyone I have ever known. She possessed two other skills that matched these: her compassion for others and her unbeatable sense of humor. I was thrilled to have Kelly join me on Diamond's case.

Unfortunately, Diamond didn't stick around long enough to meet her. By now, she had taken to a life on the street. She had run away from her first foster home within days of placement. Kelly's first official act as Diamond's CASA was to drive up and down the streets of Cincinnati looking for her. The caseworker had provided a picture of Diamond, and Kelly studied it carefully. It was a long shot that she would recognize a child she had never met, but she looked anyway. She had to do something.

Eventually, Diamond returned and Kelly made a connection. Diamond ran again and when she was ready to be found, Kelly was the person she called from an apartment in a crime-ridden part of town. Diamond didn't know the address. On that Sunday night, Mother's Day no less, Kelly climbed out of her warm bed and into her car, headed to retrieve Diamond from the forsaken place she had been.

For the next four years, Kelly remained Diamond's constant advocate. Kelly argued tirelessly for Diamond in and out of court. She reviewed potential foster homes and selected the one she thought would be the best match. She encouraged Diamond to stay in school and try out for the basketball team. She attended her games and cheered her on from the sidelines. Despite Kelly's constant involvement, Diamond struggled with school, peers, and was forever running away.

When Diamond kept running, Kelly made the difficult decision to advocate for Diamond's placement in a residential facility in Dayton, Ohio, about ninety minutes away. Here, Diamond would live with other girls who could not make it in a foster home and who were at risk to themselves or others. Diamond's endless running away and other lifestyle choices put her at risk, and Kelly couldn't bear to watch it any longer.

When Diamond moved into this facility, Kelly faithfully made the long drive to visit her frequently. At fifteen, she was not a likely candidate for adoption.

Over the course of the next three years, Kelly fought hard for Diamond. She challenged Diamond to make good choices and to take care of herself so that she could have a healthy future. Likewise, she challenged every case-worker and therapist to see Diamond's potential. In the time that Kelly was officially appointed to Diamond's case, she had seen ten different caseworkers come and go from Diamond's life.

Miraculously, at age eighteen, Diamond graduated from high school. She had come a long way from being a fourteen-year-old runaway. The fact that she graduated from high school was a huge accomplishment for a child who had run the streets for months at a time. "Over a third of foster youth earn neither a high school diploma nor a GED" (Courtney et al., 2005). As usual, Kelly was there to celebrate this milestone with her.

Being on the ProKids team as a GAL allowed me to give Diamond what she had needed so desperately years earlier: one adult who could support and advocate for her. As a CASA, Kelly filled this role quite nicely, much better than I could have as her GAL. The structure of ProKids enabled me to help Kelly help Diamond, while simultaneously helping twenty other CASAs advocate for the fifty to sixty five children we represented together. I offered Kelly suggestions and guided her in her efforts to help Diamond. Kelly and I attended court hearings together and I assisted Kelly in navigating the child welfare system on Diamond's behalf.

Diamond was eventually emancipated from the foster care system at eighteen. She moved into her own apartment and became fully self-sufficient. Kelly remained an active support to Diamond even after her court case was officially closed.

When Diamond was twenty years old, she returned to ProKids to tell her life story. It was the story that could have emerged in therapy when she was nine, or in our car rides together eleven years earlier, but never did. As she began to talk, all the noise and people around us began to fade away, and I hung onto every word that tumbled from her lips.

To say Aunt Beverly was stern would be an understatement. She was downright abusive, regularly beating Diamond with a belt, or any other object she could get her hands on. At the age of five, Diamond was feeding her mother and changing her diapers because Beverly would not. At the age of seven, when her mother died, she threw herself onto her mother's body, stricken with grief, and was knocked to the ground when Beverly pushed her away. Lost in addictions to drugs and alcohol, Beverly left her to fend for herself. In her hazy drug binges, she brought men into their home. I was shocked. With tears in my eyes, I asked her why she hadn't told me years earlier. We had spent so much time together, going to and from her therapy sessions.

"I was getting up the courage to tell you when a new driver started taking me to therapy. I wanted to tell you. I tried. But I was too scared. And then you were gone. Later when I met Kelly, I got a second chance."

Diamond's painful life had been interrupted by her CASA. Diamond's heartbreaking story gave way to hope after she met Kelly. Kelly showed her there was a different way of life and encouraged her to live it. Through all the foster homes and the residential treatment facility, Kelly was actively involved in making sure Diamond got the help she needed. Kelly spent time in Diamond's schools, talking to teachers and others, and convincing them to give Diamond all the help she needed academically to ensure she would succeed. After high school, Diamond took classes to learn how to live on her own. In these classes, she was taught how to use a washer and dryer. Kelly taught her how to use her past as a learning experience and a launching pad for a fresh start. In class, she learned how to make a budget. She learned from Kelly that she possessed the skill and strength to make a better life for herself than her aunt or the system had made for her. The system gave Diamond bits and pieces of a future. Kelly helped her put it all together in a way that made success a possibility. Kelly's desire to help children and become a CASA made all the difference in Diamond's world.

Each year thousands of children just like Diamond leave the foster care system at the age of eighteen. They have never found a family to anchor and support them. They are technically adults, though many have never had the chance to grow emotionally or to learn all the lessons necessary to allow them live on their own. Many suffer from mental illnesses such as major depression. About one fourth will be incarcerated within the first two years after they leave the system. Over one fifth will become homeless at some time after age eighteen (Courtney et al, 2005).

When Diamond was reportedly sexually abused as an eight-year-old, the system stepped up to help her. The system provided a therapist to work with her and a caseworker to ensure she received the therapy she needed. But overall, the system failed her. Why?

The system failed her because the system can't save children. Adults save children. A community saves children. The system's response to these children is bureaucratic and unnatural. The system rarely offers children like Diamond the kinds of solid relationships that protects and sustains children and allows them to heal and to grow. Although Diamond had a therapist and caseworker, she did not have an adult she could trust to take care of her.

Looking back at my involvement in Diamond's life as a Children's Services caseworker, I realize that I did the best I could with her case. It wasn't nearly enough, but the system isn't designed to guarantee that it will deliver nearly enough to the children for whom it exists. As her caseworker, I offered assistance artificially. She was abused and violated. I offered therapy. Beverly would not take her. I drove her instead. When I logistically could not get her to her appointment due to time constraints, I ensured someone else would take her. What I didn't offer was a trusted, consistent adult who could really develop an ongoing relationship with her.

Diamond is a success story. All too many children like her grow up and never leave the streets. Many have substance abuse addictions, live in poverty, and experience violence at the hands of men with whom they associate. A large number of these women bring babies into their world of abuse and chaos.

I've sat with such women who experienced abuse and neglect as a child, only to perpetuate the same for their children. I used to think that these would be the very people who would refuse to allow their children to suffer. After all, they know firsthand how devastating childhood can be. They should know better. But what I am learning is that it's hard to be a good mom when you've never had one. It's hard to know how to take care of and nurture your baby if you have never been nurtured.

When my first child was born, I had no idea what to do with her. I was surrounded with family, friends, and a husband who adored our daughter and me. One morning when Hanna was about a month old, I vividly remember sitting at the kitchen table eating a bowl of cereal while she sat in her bouncy seat beside me. She was just staring at me. It freaked me out a little. What was I supposed to do with her? She was looking at me, seemingly expecting something. Was it conversation? How in the world do you talk to a baby? What could she possibly want to talk about, anyway? She didn't seem to want to be held; she looked quite content there, watching me eat. So I continued eating my breakfast, vaguely uneasy that my infant was judging me.

Later that day we went to visit my mother, who immediately scooped Hanna out of her pumpkin seat and began talking to her. Crazy talk. Baby talk. My mother made absolutely no sense, and was actually being quite funny with her nonsensical gibberish. Hanna was delighted and I was dumb-founded. Note to self: talk like a fool and your baby will adore you.

The next day Hanna and I sat together again. She looked at me from her bouncy seat, and again, I had no idea what to do with her. Following my mother's example, I began talking to her with lots of animation and very little sense. It went against every natural instinct in my body. After all, I was a fairly intelligent, somewhat educated individual. Why was I talking nonsense to a baby? But, I did it because Hanna loved it. And I loved the way she responded to me. If my mother hadn't demonstrated that to me, Hanna and I may very well have spent her whole first year just looking at each other. Think of the speech delays she was spared!

Being a new mom made me think about all of the young mothers who raise babies on their own without any help or support in the form of family. Getting acclimated to motherhood was a major adjustment with a steep learning curve, and I had resources other new parents lacked. My mother had showered me with nurturance and affection as a child, and I did the same with my own. I experienced stability while I was growing up, and had a family dinner every night with my parents and five brothers and sisters. My husband and I pass that on to our kids.

Many of the parents I have come across in my line of work experienced abuse or neglect as a child. Many were raised in the foster care system. Nearly all of them lack any kind of support system in the form of extended family and friends. Oftentimes they suffer from substance abuse, mental illness, and poverty. Looking back into their family history there were often multiple generations that experienced the same problems, each passing on abuse and neglect as a legacy to the unborn.

In my line of work, there is a lot to be done. Casting judgment on people is not something I have the time or the energy to do. I did, however, wonder how we could break this cycle that so many families were caught in. Cases of abused and neglected children were flooding into the ProKids office rapidly. Many times, they involved infants and toddlers. If we handled these fragile and vulnerable children with great care and impeccable advocacy, could we perhaps spare them the legacy they were handed, and set them on a different course?

I believed we could. With a preschooler and a toddler at home, I learned as much as possible about the effects of abuse and neglect on very young children. The 1990s was the decade of the brain, and there was new information all the time about how early life experiences shape a developing brain and impact lifelong capacities for cognitive development and important emotional growth.

In 2000, after being at ProKids for two years, I created a program called Building Blocks: Specialized Advocacy for Abused and Neglected Infants and Toddlers. I had seen the way CASAs like Kelly changed the lives of children like Diamond. I knew CASAs could have an even greater impact on very young children if they were trained on the special needs of babies and toddlers. I knew that CASAs held the best chance of impacting those little lives, as well as the lives of subsequent generations.

I had relatively simple goals for ProKids Building Blocks when it began. First, it was critical that CASAs be trained on issues relating to young children and how to spot signs of trouble relating to physical development, emotional growth, and daily care. Second, every Building Blocks CASA needed to conduct frequent home visits. ProKids required CASAs to visit children once per month. Building Blocks CASAs are required to complete visits twice per month, and must visit each location where the child spends a significant amount of time, such as a babysitter's home or childcare center. Third, Building Blocks CASAs need to be familiar with services offered to young children, such as early intervention programs, in order to address developmental delays and offer therapeutic services to assist in the development of an emotionally healthy relationship between a child and caregiver.

In 2000, I could not locate any advocacy programs like Building Blocks. Realizing I would have to start at ground level, I drew on the expertise of various professionals I had met over the course of my career. One by one, incredibly talented and passionate people stepped up to help with program development. Building Blocks advisors included social workers along with a pediatrician, dentist, obstetrician, child psychologist, juvenile court magistrate, and Kelly, Diamond's CASA. Together we developed a training curriculum and home visitation checklists which CASAs complete following home visits. With the help of the advisors and other expert professionals, CASA training is conducted twice per year.

In addition to developing and providing the training, the advisors brought their experiences and concerns to the table. One advisor, an adoptive mother, suggested that CASAs be required to take photos of the children regularly in order to document their early lives. She talked about how difficult it was for adopted children when they were told to bring their baby pictures to school for a project or other reasons. For many adopted children, there are no such photos. The magistrate also noted that photos would make the children appear more real to magistrates who never see them otherwise. As a result, CASAs take pictures of children regularly and supply them intermittently to the court. When a case is closed, the pictures are given to the person who has custody of the child. Photos are also shared with biological parents and relatives, who often do not have a single picture of their children.

It always amazes me how biological parents react when a CASA offers them a picture of their child. Many parents are struck by this simple act, and it powerfully fosters a good working relationship. Violet was a twenty-eight-year-old mother with a heroin addiction. Her son, Manny, was a year old and living in foster care while she underwent drug treatment. She was impossibly difficult to engage. She was angry with everyone and everything. Manny's

CASA, John, approached Violet prior to a court hearing and offered her a small booklet filled with pictures of Manny that he had taken on his various visits to Manny's foster home. Violet eyed him with suspicion and slowly opened the album. Her rigid, angry body relaxed as she studied each photo carefully. When she was through and John told her she could have it, she was nearly speechless. This small album opened the door to the first productive conversation John and Violet had.

Another advisor, a pediatrician, offered to consult on cases involving medical issues and attend home visits along with CASAs when they had concerns related to the health or development of a child. She has reviewed medical records and offered suggestions on how to follow up with concerns.

Within months, we trained a core group of CASAs who were assigned to infants and toddlers. Looking back, the least challenging parts of my job were finding volunteers to commit to the additional training and advocacy and finding the right professionals to help develop the program. Those pieces fell into place nearly effortlessly, as if the program was meant to be. The hardest part of all was getting other system professionals, such as caseworkers, attorneys, and magistrates to understand how critical it was that we begin to see babies and toddlers in the light of scientific research as it related to the first three years of life and critical brain development.

I quickly learned that my responsibilities went far beyond understanding the needs of infants and toddlers and helping CASAs advocate successfully for young children. My greater task was to dispel the myths that babies and toddlers are not deeply affected by exposure to family violence, multiple moves between foster homes, and sporadic visitation with biological parents who refuse to change their abusive or neglectful behavior.

When older children are suffering and cannot make sense of what is happening to them, they sometimes lash out at themselves and everyone around them. Many who are extremely troubled experience alarming behavior problems such as fire setting or killing small animals. They disrupt classrooms and threaten teachers. They demand a lot of attention.

Babies and young children are not able to demand this attention. They do not have the size or strength to do so. As a result, they remain largely unseen by the professionals working in the system who are busy responding to troubled, older children. But as maltreated babies grow, so do their problems. Our small window of opportunity to help them begins to close very quickly.

Abused and neglected young children are faced with a double whammy. Not only do they lack the size and strength to demand attention, too many professionals assigned to help them do not know how to read their cues for help. Their last chance may be a professional who is able to read between the lines of their little lives.

We used to believe that babies didn't have language. After all, they do not use words to communicate. I have learned that they indeed have language and we need to begin learning it. Babies cannot tell caseworkers with words that they are distressed. Instead, they often experience difficulty regulating their little bodies. They may sleep far too much or far too little. They may have gastrointestinal distress or feeding problems. In order to understand how they are faring in foster care, professionals need to learn to read babies. They can tell us a lot about their lives, if we only know how to listen.

Several years after I began ProKids Building Blocks, a CASA and I were assigned to a little boy. Donald was eighteen months old and his mother was sixteen. She had been in foster care for many years and had never been adopted. She suffered from a variety of mental health diagnoses, including Reactive Attachment Disorder and major depression. She had lived in as many as seven different foster homes with her young son since his birth.

As I watched him scoot around on the floor of the foster home, I was struck by his behavior. He did not pay a bit of attention to his mother and would not look her in the eye. When he fell down and bumped his head, he went to the CASA, a total stranger, for reassurance instead of his mother. He was significantly developmentally delayed and his mother was vague regarding any prior medical care. I sensed that he had remained unseen by not only his mother, but also by the caseworkers and other professionals who paraded through their lives. Each time his mother disrupted a foster placement because of her behavior, he was packed up right along with her things, and moved into the next home. He was in trouble.

Fortunately, his CASA, Heather, was a trained Building Blocks CASA and immediately set about helping this little boy. She researched his medical records and found that his immunizations were not up-to-date. She advocated for early intervention services and ensured he began physical, occupational, and speech therapy to address his delays. She consulted with an infant mental health therapist and arranged for weekly therapy to begin. Donald and his mother attended therapy together each week where the therapist worked with them on strengthening their bonding and attachment. After ten sessions with Donald and his mother, the therapist noted her concerns regarding his mother's self-absorbed behavior and inability to see Donald as a separate person with significant emotional and physical needs.

One day Donald's mother ran away from her foster home, taking him with her. They were found two days later at her boyfriend's home, where three adults, along with his mother, were smoking crack cocaine. Donald was sitting on the floor, playing with an empty water bottle.

Children's Services removed Donald from his mother and placed him in a foster home. Heather went to visit him at his new foster home and monitored his placement and every aspect of his care while he was there. A new caseworker was assigned, and in the transition, information regarding his physical, occupational, and speech therapies was lost. Heather bridged the gap, and due to her efforts, those services continued without disruption.

In the meantime, Donald's mother entered a drug treatment program in which he could live with her. Although Heather was a strong advocate for families, she felt it was in Donald's best interest to remain in the foster home. Heather believed his mother needed to make progress resolving her own problems before Donald was uprooted again. He desperately needed the stability his foster home offered. Although the new caseworker disagreed, the magistrate ruled that Donald would remain in his foster home while his mother underwent drug treatment.

Three months later, Donald's mother left the drug treatment facility, and could not be found. Heather recommended that the court move forward with terminating Donald's mother's rights and seeking adoption. Donald was two years old at this point, and should not spend any more time waiting for his mother to be able and willing to take care of him.

Despite her best efforts at achieving permanency in a timely manner, the turnover in caseworkers and court continuances resulted in the trial being drawn out over another year. Although Donald was doing well in his foster home, his foster parents did not wish to adopt him. As a result, Heather advocated for him to be placed in a foster home that would adopt him when he became available. The Children's Services caseworker insisted there were no homes available that would be willing to foster Donald with the intention of adopting him later.

When Heather and I were told that there were no foster-to-adopt homes for Donald, I knew it wasn't true. In fact, just a year before, I had been the GAL for two little girls who were adopted by a wonderful family. They had wanted to adopt a son as well. I contacted them and learned they were interested in adopting a little boy and had been licensed for both foster care and adoption. Heather and I presented this as an option for Donald, and after careful planning and visitation with this family, Donald moved into their home.

At the age of five, after the court granted termination of parental rights, this family adopted Donald. He had been living in their home for eighteen months at the time of his adoption finalization. Heather's gift to the family included all the pictures she had taken of Donald from the time she first met him at eighteen months. She was not only his advocate, but also the historian of his early life.

Each and every day, CASAs like John and Heather change the direction of little lives. I have seen it repeatedly. It is so easy for children like Donald to remain unnoticed until they reach preschool and kindergarten and simply cannot function. We don't see them until they are big enough and strong enough to demand control of a classroom. By then, we have missed a window of opportunity that we cannot recover.

CASAs not only change the course of little lives. Their attention to detail has saved some as well. Building Blocks CASAs pay attention to the minute details that caseworkers and others may miss. For example, one day a CASA named Ann made a foster home visit to see three-month-old Jolene. She paused outside the house after she noticed the foster mother's car in the driveway and the baby's car seat strapped into the front passenger side. During her home visit, Ann discussed car seat safety with Jolene's foster mother. She explained that the safest place for Jolene to be transported was in the middle of the backseat. She suggested that the local fire department could assist her in ensuring the car seat was safely mounted and encouraged the foster mother to have this done. Fortunately, the foster mother took Ann's advice and followed through. The very next week, the foster family was involved in a fatal car accident. The driver of the other car was killed. Jolene, safely restrained, escaped unharmed.

Over the past eight years, ProKids Building Blocks has served hundreds of infants and toddlers. We will probably never know the far-reaching effects of our CASAs' advocacy. What we do know is that in 2007, 100% of these children did not experience a recurrence of abuse or neglect (ProKids, 2007). This is a phenomenal accomplishment, given infants and toddlers in foster care are more likely to be abused and neglected than children in the general population. Amazingly, 76% of these children resided with siblings at the time of court termination (ProKids, 2007). Far too often, children in foster care lose their siblings along with everything familiar to them. In a system where more than half of the infants and toddlers in foster care have untreated developmental delays, 99% of young children served by a Building Blocks CASA achieved developmental milestones or were receiving services to help them catch up (ProKids, 2007).

At ProKids, we have found a little goes a long way.

CHAPTER 9

A Little Goes
a Long Way

FIFTEEN-MONTH-OLD KIESHA HAD BEEN living with her twenty-three year-old mother, Lucinda, since she was born. Lucinda was significantly depressed, living in poverty and fighting a losing battle with an addiction to cocaine. She was facing eviction, and the night before, had engaged in a shouting match with her boyfriend, which had escalated to punches thrown in all directions as Kiesha curled up in a fetal position in her playpen. The next morning, Lucinda woke to the sound of Kiesha crying, still in her playpen, her diaper soaked and her little t-shirt stained with vomit. Her boyfriend long gone, Lucinda picked up her crying baby and began to cry herself. She just couldn't go on anymore and Kiesha couldn't live like this either. Somewhere between the tears of the two mingling together, Lucinda made her decision.

She absent-mindedly threw together some of Kiesha's clothes, a couple of diapers, and an old blanket. She scooped her up and boarded a bus, heading for downtown. The bus wound through the city streets. Kiesha sat on her mom's lap, sucking on her pacifier and looking out the window. They stepped off the bus when it stopped outside the local Children's Services agency. Lucinda pushed open the doors and passed through the metal detector. Her eyes scanned the information board, looking for the right floor. The ding of the elevator announced her arrival to Children's Services, the place where she would leave her baby behind. She paused for just a second when she took a deep breath and pushed herself out of the elevator.

A caseworker named Melissa emerged from behind closed doors. She and Lucinda talked about what had brought Lucinda to the office that day. Lucinda told the caseworker she just couldn't be a mom anymore. She couldn't do it. She was behind on her rent, out of food, and never wanted to get out of bed. Melissa suggested they meet with a team of caseworkers and try to work together to find a way to help the little girl and her mother. Melissa and her co-workers offered Lucinda emergency housing assistance and a voucher for food. Lucinda said no. They offered childcare assistance so she could get a break during the day. No. They offered her mental health treatment and a mental health caseworker who would work with her intensively and be available by pager 24 hours a day. Again, no.

Finally, Lucinda divulged that cocaine was the only thing that made her feel better. The caseworkers offered to place her in a drug treatment program where Kiesha could live with her. Arrangements could be made that day. "No," Lucinda said.

She was done.

The caseworkers asked about extended family support. Lucinda's mother was an alcoholic and her father was dead. She did not have brothers or sisters. She had not seen Kiesha's father since the night she told him she was pregnant. She had no idea where he was or if he had any family members. Melissa explained that Lucinda would need to sign a paper giving custody to the Children's Services Agency for a period of thirty days, during which time the case would be opened in court. She would be notified of the day and time of the hearing regarding her daughter.

"Show me where to sign," she said.

Lucinda was done. She just couldn't put her daughter through the kind of life she had lived. There was no going back now. She signed the piece of paper, handed over her sleeping baby, and kissed her on the forehead. Her face stoic, she hurried out the door.

When Kiesha awoke, she was sitting on the lap of a caseworker. She immediately reached for her pacifier, which was clipped to the front of her stained t-shirt. She put it in her mouth and laid her head back on the caseworker while she took in the sights around her. When another caseworker appeared with juice and crackers and offered them to her, Kiesha clumsily attempted to get them from her little fist into her mouth. She could not move her hands fast enough to get the food into her aching stomach.

While one caseworker set about calling foster homes that would be available right away, another went to look for the few toys that were kept at the office for times like these. Melissa began to dig through the bag Kiesha had arrived with, hoping to find some clean clothes. The clothes inside were two sizes too small. Melissa went to find any clean clothes in the office that might fit Kiesha. The closet, which held items for such emergencies, was nearly bare. Melissa was lucky enough to find a sleeper twice Kiesha's size, but it would do. Then, she called her husband to tell him she would be working late that night.

Within hours, Melissa was driving Kiesha across town to her new foster home. Kiesha sat in the back, strapped in a car seat, sucking her pacifier, and looking out the window.

One Monday morning several weeks later, I arrived in court to appear on new cases. I signed in and received the paperwork. One of the complaints involved Kiesha. I read the entire complaint to get a more thorough understanding of my new responsibility.

The hearing was over in twenty minutes. Melissa testified to the facts concerning the day Lucinda brought Kiesha to Children's Services. Melissa had driven out to Lucinda's apartment to tell her about the court hearing. Lucinda told her that she would be at court, but she did not appear. The judge granted interim custody of Kiesha to Children's Services, allowing her placement in foster care to continue. Trial dates were set three months out to determine what services would be required for Lucinda to reunify, or whether relative care or adoption would be in her best interests.

Following the hearing, Melissa filled me in on the day Lucinda had come into their office. She passed on the name and phone number of the foster home and the little information she had about Kiesha's early life. She stated Kiesha was doing well in her foster home. Melissa then introduced me to Mike, the new caseworker who would be replacing her. Because Melissa was from an intake unit, Kiesha's case would be transferred to a new, ongoing caseworker who would oversee the case.

My first task involved assigning a CASA to Kiesha's case. Susan came to mind. She had been a Building Blocks CASA for several years and had advocated successfully for eleven young children in that time. She was a nurse by trade and had come to volunteer at ProKids when her youngest child started high school. When I called Susan to talk to her about Kiesha's case, she didn't hesitate before agreeing to take it.

Later that day, I called Kiesha's foster mother to introduce myself and schedule a home visit for Susan and me. Our schedules were difficult to align. Kiesha's foster mother was a single parent and worked full time, making evening or weekend visits a necessity. Her weekends were also busy. She and Kiesha would only be home one evening between 5:30 and 6:30 p.m. I penciled them in and called Susan to confirm.

Susan and I arrived for our visit. The foster mother greeted us at the door and invited us into the living room. The small, red brick home was clean and pleasant. I looked around for signs indicating a baby lived there. The only visible indication of a baby in the house was the playpen tucked into the corner of the living room. Inside the playpen sat an adorable little girl. Her hair was neatly braided and she was dressed in a pretty pink and white sundress. She sat quietly with a couple of toys. She looked up at Susan and me, and immediately looked away, back at her fingers as they rubbed a stuffed animal.

Her foster mother invited Susan and me to sit while she retrieved Kiesha from her playpen. Kiesha had just put her pacifier in her mouth when her foster mother grabbed it and put it on the coffee table in front of us. "I've been trying to break her of that nasty habit."

Kiesha blinked her big brown eyes a couple of times, but otherwise did not respond. The pacifier sat on the coffee table amidst a number of small glass knick-knacks.

As her foster mother continued talking, I watched Kiesha and how she responded to the adults around her. Something just wasn't right. She sat so still on the couch that I hardly knew she was there. She seemed to have learned how not to be seen or heard. Her foster mother, Susan, and I talked about how she was settling into the foster home.

Her foster mother told us, "She's no trouble. She's a really good baby. You hardly know she's here."

I explained my role as GAL and Susan's role as CASA, and then took a backseat to Susan as she engaged the foster mother in a deeper conversation about how things were going. Susan asked questions about Kiesha's physical development, how she was sleeping and eating, and how she related to the other children in the home. Susan got the same answer each time. Fine, just fine. On the surface, Kiesha looked fine, just fine, but something wasn't right.

Susan asked about Kiesha's medical care. Did the foster mother have her immunization records? Had she been to the doctor since her foster care placement? The foster mother had taken her to a pediatrician, but did not have any medical history with her. "She probably didn't have any immunizations. We'll just have to do them all over again," the foster mother stated.

The questions about Kiesha's medical care continued. Was the foster mother given any information about her medical history? Does she have any outstanding medical issues that we need to be aware of? I had hoped the caseworker passed such information along to the foster parents, but the foster mother didn't know. Many young children in foster care have significant delays. Susan asked the foster mother whether she had any concerns about how Kiesha was growing. The foster mother responded that Kiesha wasn't very active. In addition, she didn't make much noise, except to cry when she didn't get her way.

Susan and I talked with her about the possibility of developmental delays and the necessity of referring Kiesha for an assessment to determine whether she was experiencing problems with her physical growth. Her foster mother was concerned about having time to participate in such evaluations. Her work schedule did not allow her the flexibility to take time off during the day. We reassured her that a team of professionals could arrange a time convenient for her and would conduct the assessment in her home. If she needed ongoing services, the service providers could work with Kiesha at the babysitter's home or wherever Kiesha was available to receive help.

Susan asked the foster mother if she had any questions or if there was anything else she wanted to talk about. She had only one issue. "I need respite care. My daughter plays soccer on a select team and we travel all over for her games. I need respite care for Kiesha for the next three weekends."

I talked with her about how difficult this could be for Kiesha, who was trying to get settled into a new home and a new routine. Her foster mom reported that there was nothing else she could do, she had been fostering children for twenty years, and really didn't want to continue. She agreed to Kiesha's placement because a caseworker begged her to take her. There was a shortage of foster homes, and Kiesha needed to go somewhere else.

Susan and the foster mother were wrapping up their conversation when I caught sight of Kiesha looking at me out of the corner of her eye. I talked to her, hoping she would show some reaction. She didn't. During our hour-long visit, neither Susan nor I saw any hint of emotion from Kiesha.

On the surface Kiesha looked fine, just fine. She was clean and well dressed. She looked healthy enough. She wasn't crying or screaming. If I had conducted the exact same home visit when I was a young, inexperienced caseworker, I would have left feeling good about what I had seen. This is precisely why young children like Kiesha get pushed to the back of the critical list when caseworkers have older, troubled children to attend to.

Although Kiesha physically looked OK, she was far from fine. She had come into foster care after being exposed to domestic violence. She was likely neglected and experiencing significant developmental delays. Through her eyes, the world was a big, scary place where she was helpless and on her own. Her lack of emotion indicated that she was shutting down. Her arrival in foster care initiated an endless stream of different people who took care of her. From day to day, she did not know what to expect. Perhaps somewhere in the depths of her little brain, she decided it was better not to expect anything.

The brown-eyed toddler with braided hair and the cute little pink and white sundress faced an uncertain future. She did not have any concept of family, who she was, or to whom she belonged. Trouble was brewing beneath the surface of the clean, well-dressed little girl. Untreated, it had the potential to grow and wreak havoc on all aspects of Kiesha's future, including her ability to learn and participate in meaningful relationships with others.

Thankfully, we now have professionals who understand the language and behaviors of very young children. We used to believe that babies didn't know the difference between caregivers. We thought that babies were interested only in eating and sleeping. We used to believe that young children were "resilient" and could automatically move beyond trauma and loss. We now know that even very young children who have suffered abuse and neglect, loss and trauma benefit from professional help.

This shift in awareness has led to changes in the way these children are seen by mental health professionals. Responding to what is being learned about babies and toddlers from research, a group of dedicated professionals created the World Association for Infant Mental Health, a grassroots effort to raise awareness of the emotional needs of very young children. This relatively new discipline emerged out of a growing body of evidence, supporting the belief that early life experiences shape long-term well being.

"Infant mental health is developing the capacity of the child from birth to age three to experience, regulate and express emotions; form close and secure interpersonal relationships; and explore the environment and learn-all in the context of family, community and cultural expectations for young children" (Zero To Three, 2003). When very young children struggle with emotions such as frustration, anger, and fear, they rely on adults to help them manage. They need to be soothed and reassured. They need to feel like someone bigger than they are is in charge and can help them. When adults fail, through abuse or neglect, young children are left to sort it all out on their own, a task that is impossible for their developing brains.

Unfortunately, infant mental health is sometimes confused with infant mental illness. There is no such thing as infant mental illness. The field of infant mental health actively works to support the healthy emotional growth and development of children to prevent mental illness later in life.

In creating the Building Blocks program at ProKids, I researched services available for infants and toddlers who experienced chaos and trauma in their early lives. This research led me to the Young Child Institute, a small program within a larger agency called Central Clinic in Cincinnati, Ohio. I had never heard of it before, or utilized it for children on my caseload, despite working in the child welfare system for years. Therapists at the Young Child Institute work with young children and their parents on developing a healthy and positive relationship with one another.

When I spoke to the director of the Young Child Institute for the first time, she explained that her staff typically worked with children who were at risk of emotional problems due to experiencing disruptions in attachments to adult caregivers. Many of their referrals were coming from Cincinnati Children's Hospital and involved helping young children who had been hospitalized for lengthy periods of time. These children needed help transitioning back home to their families. I asked if they had worked with young foster children, as these children had suffered abuse, neglect, and separation from all that was familiar to them. Quite honestly, she answered that they kept busy enough without seeking new referrals. Besides, the foster children they had worked with were difficult to help. Caseworkers frequently did not return phone calls, and their therapists were never notified when children had changed homes. They simply were gone, without any notice, and with no forwarding contact information.

Over time, my conversations with the director continued, and she began teaching me a great deal about young children and how they can be helped. One by one, she dispelled the myths related to what goes on inside the developing mind and body of a young child who has not had the experience of a loving, consistent relationship with a nurturing adult. These children are, in fact, deeply affected by their experiences. The good news is that with the right therapeutic intervention, and at least the presence of at least one committed adult, these children can and will heal.

Within just a couple of weeks, Kiesha's CASA, Susan, realized that Kiesha could not stay in her current foster home. Susan was concerned about the number of times Kiesha would go to different foster homes for respite care while the foster family traveled. Additionally, Kiesha was left with different babysitters during the week while the foster mother worked. Given her history of moving around, it was in Kiesha's best interests to get into a home and be able to stay there, so she could begin making sense of this world that changed constantly and had been brutal to her. Moving children from one home to another is a decision not to be made lightly. Susan made every effort to prevent multiple moves for children. However, if Kiesha stayed where she was, she would make countless moves each week and each weekend, exacerbating her growing problem of finding security and attachment to a consistent adult caregiver.

Although Mike, Kiesha's new Children's Services caseworker, understood Susan's concerns about the foster home situation, he stated that there was really nothing that could be done differently. There are no rules against foster parents using different babysitters and accessing respite care frequently. Mike believed he had to accept the home that was chosen for Kiesha. Susan believed it was critical to obtain stability for the petite toddler with big brown eyes. In a court hearing two weeks later, Susan voiced her concerns to the magistrate, and at that time, all parties agreed to find a more stable living situation for Kiesha. Mike had already referred Kiesha for a full developmental evaluation and the date for the assessment was pending.

Within days, a new foster home had been located for Kiesha. The foster parents, Jim and Brenda, had two biological sons, ages twelve and nine, and a four-year-old foster daughter. Jim worked full time and Brenda worked two days per week. Brenda's mother babysat the kids in the foster home while she worked. Her background checks were completed, and she was approved as a respite caregiver for foster children. On the rare occasions when the family traveled, they took all of the children with them. When Kiesha's first foster mother learned that a new home had been found, she asked for Kiesha's immediate removal from her home. She didn't have the time or desire to help her transition to this new home after a series of pre-placement visits.

Later that afternoon, Mike drove out to Kiesha's foster home and loaded her, along with the usual black trash bag packed with her clothes, into his car. Kiesha sat in a car seat, clutching a small blanket and sucking on her pacifier.

The very next morning, Susan arrived at the new foster home to see how Kiesha was settling in. She was relieved to find the home pleasant and had an air of easiness. Children's artwork was framed throughout the home, and a large wall in the living room was devoted to pictures of each of the foster children that lived there over the years. Kiesha sat on the floor of the living room, absorbed in building a tower of blocks. She would get three stacked and they would crash down, much to her amazement. Then she would begin again. Kiesha's new foster parents were delightful people who seemed committed to children, both their own and the foster children who came through their front door.

Although she was pleased with Kiesha's new foster home, Susan continued to be concerned about the multiple moves and caregivers Kiesha had experienced in her short life. Kiesha did not make eye contact with anyone, and preferred to always be left alone. Her foster mother reported that she did not nap during the day, and would lay awake in bed for hours before falling asleep. Susan spoke to the caseworker and foster parents about these concerns and requested that a referral to the Young Child Institute for therapy be made.

Soon thereafter, Kiesha was scheduled for an intake appointment with a therapist. Kiesha and her foster mother appeared for the appointment, along with Susan and Mike. Together they discussed the concerns about Kiesha's withdrawn behavior, her disrupted sleep patterns, and her willingness to go with strangers. The therapist gathered information about what brought Kiesha into foster care and what the long-term plans were for her placement. Kiesha's foster mother was willing to attend weekly sessions with Kiesha. It is not possible to do therapy with a young child unless there is an adult caregiver actively participating. At the conclusion of the intake appointment, the therapist determined that Kiesha could benefit from weekly therapy, and sessions were scheduled.

With Kiesha living in a good environment and therapeutic interventions beginning, Susan set her sights on the remaining tasks before her. Hoping to find Lucinda, she drove out to her apartment and left a note, asking Lucinda to call her. She wanted to meet and gather more information about her, as well as information about any potential relatives. Susan then called every medical clinic in the area, searching for any records that might belong to Kiesha. On her seventh try, she hit the jackpot. She located the clinic where Lucinda had taken Kiesha for sporadic medical care. She had a smattering of immunizations, but was quite behind.

Susan passed all of this information onto the caseworker and ensured that Kiesha's new doctor was aware of her history. At her next medical appointment, her new pediatrician reviewed her prior records and noted that she was small in size and height for her age, but was gaining significantly in both areas since her foster care placement.

It is important to note that although caseworkers are ultimately responsible for things like securing medical records, many of them struggle to find time to conduct the amount of investigation it sometimes takes to retrieve them. Kiesha's CASA, Susan, had only two cases at the time, giving her a lot more time and energy to devote to thoroughly investigating every aspect of those cases. Furthermore, she and Mike worked well together as a team and passed information back and forth regularly, which helped a great deal when it came time to make recommendations to the court.

Several months later, Susan received a call from Kiesha's caseworker. Mike had new information. Lucinda was living in a homeless shelter downtown and wanted services to reunify with her daughter. She had requested visitation, which was her right. Mike suggested that Lucinda meet with both him and Susan to discuss services and visitation. Lucinda agreed.

Susan was not sure what to expect as she and Mike waited for Lucinda to arrive for their scheduled meeting. Would Lucinda be angry and demanding? Would she be remorseful and sad that she had not seen her daughter in over six months? Would she appear at all?

Lucinda did in fact appear for their appointment. She was dressed from head to toe in blue denim and looked a decade older than she actually was. Her face was drawn and her eyes were hollow. She was bone thin, her belt wrapped twice around her waist to hold up her torn jeans. She had hit rock bottom and knew it. She had been smoking marijuana regularly since she was fourteen and reported feeling very overwhelmed and depressed after Kiesha was born. She had no family support and tried to make it on her own when she hooked up with a boyfriend who turned her onto cocaine. His angry fists turned on her as well, and he began beating her and threatened to kill her. Her own childhood history was filled with abuse and neglect. Her mother was an alcoholic and blamed her for her father's death when she was nine.

The conversation turned to Kiesha and how she was doing. Lucinda wanted to know everything. Mike and Susan told her truthfully that they were concerned about her early on, but that she was making great progress in her foster home. They updated her on Keisha's progress, and told her that she was receiving speech and physical therapies to address her delays. Her language had developed from two or three words to over a hundred. She had learned to crawl, then walk, and every day seemed to be gaining new skills. She was happy and thriving with the family that was taking care of her. Additionally, she and her foster mother attended therapy each week to help Kiesha learn how to interact and trust the adult who was taking care of her. With lots of help, Kiesha was developing a sense of a world that could be trusted to help her, giving her the freedom to try new things, such as exploring her surroundings and counting on her foster mother to comfort her when she was scared or hurt.

Susan wanted to know why Lucinda had waited six months before coming forward and seeking the return of Kiesha. Lucinda replied that it was just too painful, even though she carried a picture of Kiesha with her and looked at it every day.

Mike and Susan talked with Lucinda about the long road ahead of her if she wanted to reunify with her daughter. She would need to complete a substance abuse assessment and follow through with recommendations. She would need to attend weekly therapy, obtain stable housing, and an income, and deal with her history of being a victim of domestic violence. Most importantly, she would need to participate in Kiesha's weekly therapy at Young Child Institute in order to develop a strong and loving relationship with her daughter. Lucinda agreed.

Susan gave Lucinda a picture of Kiesha that she had taken the month before. Lucinda studied the picture carefully. Tears of pain welled up in her hollow eyes. Susan wasn't sure at that moment whether Lucinda would walk away again or step up and see things through. Time would tell.

Within two weeks, Lucinda had completed a substance abuse assessment and had entered a ninety-day inpatient drug treatment facility. While there, she engaged in mental health therapy as well to address depression.

Susan and Mike contacted Kiesha's therapist to tell her about Lucinda's appearance and stated intentions. The therapist felt it was important for Lucinda to demonstrate her commitment prior to becoming part of Kiesha's weekly therapy sessions. She did not want to re-introduce Kiesha to her mother before she began addressing her substance abuse addiction. It would be detrimental to Kiesha to begin working with her mother, only to have her fail to follow through.

Lucinda was entitled to weekly visitation with Kiesha. Mike and Susan looked to the Young Child Institute therapist for her recommendation on how the visits should be structured, and how Kiesha could be prepared for seeing her mother again after so long. Would Kiesha even know her?

Mike, Susan, and the therapist agreed that visits between Kiesha and her mother would occur weekly, at Children's Services and under supervision. By now, Lucinda had completed her first thirty days of inpatient drug treatment, and was permitted passes to leave the facility for visits with Kiesha, with the caseworker's verification and approval. Luckily, Kiesha's foster mother was willing to transport Kiesha to and from the visits. She did not want Kiesha to be taken to and from the visits by a case-aide or a driver from Children's Services. She knew the visits would be confusing for Kiesha and wanted to minimize the number of adults involved.

At the recommendation of the therapist, Susan obtained a picture of Lucinda and passed it on to the foster mother, who then showed it to Kiesha and explained that she was going to visit her mama. At first Kiesha shook her head, and said, "You Mama." Her foster mother told her that some children had more than one mama, and that she was Mama Brenda, but there was another Mama, Lucinda, who wanted to see her. Kiesha just looked at her.

With the help of the therapist, Kiesha's foster mother made a picture book of a little girl going back and forth between visits. The book explained how Kiesha would get up in the morning, have her favorite breakfast of Cheerios and orange slices, and then play with her toys and her foster sister. Before lunch, she would pack her favorite Dora the Explorer backpack with her blanket, her stuffed fish, and the book Mama Brenda made with the therapist. Kiesha would get into the car with Mama Brenda and drive to a place where she would see Mama Lucinda. Mama Brenda would leave her there, but would come back for her. That night, they would have chicken nuggets for dinner, Kiesha's favorite food. After reading the book every evening for several nights, the visit day arrived.

Lucinda was nervous for her first visit with the baby she had brought into the world, but hadn't seen for nearly seven months. Mama Brenda dropped Kiesha off at the visitation center with the visit supervisor who would monitor Lucinda's visit, and handed her a diaper bag filled with spare diapers, healthy snacks, and a sippy cup. She left without meeting Lucinda.

Kiesha walked into the room holding hands with the visitation supervisor, her little Dora the Explorer backpack on her back. Lucinda cried when she saw how big her little girl had gotten. By now, Kiesha was almost two years old. Lucinda held her arms out to Kiesha. Kiesha didn't move, not quite sure what to expect, or what to do.

The two-hour visit flew by for Lucinda. Kiesha preferred to explore the toys and books on her own. Though it broke Lucinda's heart, she sat back and followed Kiesha's lead. She didn't force her onto her lap or smother her with tears and kisses. Eventually, Kiesha brought her the book Mama Brenda had made, and Lucinda read it to her. Then again, and again. When it was time to leave Lucinda hugged Kiesha tightly, though Kiesha didn't hug her back. They would return next week to visit again.

When the visit was over, the supervisor walked Kiesha out to greet Mama Brenda. Kiesha ran toward her and jumped into her arms. She placed her in the car seat and drove home. Within minutes, Kiesha fell sound asleep and was carried to her bed without waking. The visit had exhausted her. She slept for three hours, and woke just in time for her favorite dinner with her foster family.

The weekly, two-hour visits continued. Kiesha began having more temper tantrums before and after the visits. She seemed angry at times, confused, and was easily frustrated. Mama Brenda and the therapist talked about this during the weekly therapy sessions. Reintroducing Lucinda into Kiesha's life was a major change for a toddler. Some of her behavior was to be expected.

Lucinda completed her substance abuse treatment successfully and had transitioned to outpatient treatment three times a week, which also included individual therapy.

After six weeks of regular visits, Lucinda met with Kiesha's therapist to talk about Kiesha and the issues she faced. Although she was thriving, she was also experiencing confusion and sadness. They spoke about Lucinda's experience with mothering, what it was like to raise Kiesha until the age of almost one, and what led her to decide to place her in foster care. They discussed Lucinda's life experiences and how they impacted her as a mother. Over the course of this conversation, the therapist determined it was important to begin working with Lucinda and Kiesha in weekly therapy sessions. Lucinda appeared to have the insight and ability to participate effectively in therapy with Kiesha. She appeared motivated and genuine in her desire to raise her daughter. The therapy would begin to help grow a solid relationship between Kiesha and her mother. The success of this intervention was the most critical part of the reunification plan.

The therapist discussed her plans with the foster mother, Mike, and Susan and they all agreed. Mama Brenda was supportive of Lucinda's plan to reunify with Kiesha and wanted them to be successful. The therapist wisely offered to meet with Lucinda and the foster mother, in efforts to facilitate communication between them regarding Kiesha, her likes and dislikes, and her routines and schedules. With the therapist's careful facilitation, Lucinda and the foster mother began developing a relationship as well. This proved to be invaluable.

Once Lucinda began weekly therapy with Kiesha, the thrust of the work was encouraging Kiesha to develop a trusting relationship with her mother. As part of the sessions, the therapist videotaped their interaction and then reviewed it with Lucinda, identifying positive aspects of the interaction as well as areas where problems in the relationship were revealed.

Over time, Kiesha began to seek out Mama Lucinda for support and help in the sessions. Previously, when she needed help putting a puzzle together, she would bring it to the therapist. Gradually, she began looking to Lucinda for assistance. In the simplest of interactions, connections between the two began to be made and their affection for each other grew.

Lucinda applied for government housing and obtained an apartment at a reduced rate. Her Children's Services caseworker provided a voucher for her deposit and first month's rent. She successfully completed outpatient treatment and continued attending Alcoholics Anonymous (AA) or Narcotics Anonymous (NA) meetings several times per week.

As the therapy between Lucinda and her daughter continued and the relationship was strengthened, the team of professionals involved began looking toward increasing visitation. Mike and Susan visited Lucinda's new apartment and found it to be appropriate for the visits. Susan arranged donations of furniture and baby items to be delivered to Lucinda's new place. Lucinda was grateful for the support and anxious to begin weekly visits in her home, just the two of them.

The foster mother did her part as well. She transported Kiesha to and from these visits and left Lucinda her phone number in case she needed anything. Day visits went well, and so were expanded to overnights, then weekends.

Throughout this time, the therapist continued weekly sessions with Kiesha and her mother. It was not always easy for Lucinda and her daughter. It was painful for Lucinda to hear her daughter cry for Mama Brenda at night. It was also painful to watch her daughter cry for her when Mama Brenda picked her up at the end of their visit. Even so, she stayed focused on loving her daughter and taking care of business, including attending AA/NA meetings daily and working full time. She kept her own individual therapy appointments and was prescribed an anti-depressant.

Weekend visitation continued successfully for two months when the parties returned to court and agreed to Kiesha's reunification with her mother. Lucinda had successfully completed all the services the court had required her to do including drug treatment, individual therapy to address her depression and past victimization, and medication. She had maintained housing and employment and had engaged in weekly therapy with Kiesha.

Most of the services continued and Kiesha's therapist proved to be a solid support for Lucinda and her daughter. Additionally, Mama

Brenda remained involved in their lives as a support for them both. When Lucinda was ill with the flu, Mama Brenda arrived at her apartment to take Kiesha for a few days while Lucinda recovered. Susan and Mike remained involved to monitor the reunification and support them whenever possible.

Six months later, the court terminated its oversight of the case and Susan's work as Kiesha's CASA was done. Although Susan was technically finished with the case, she was always a phone call away. Once, Lucinda called with questions about finding a good childcare center. Once, she asked for advice regarding a dispute she was having with her landlord. Nonetheless, Lucinda and Kiesha were doing well. Mike kept the case open within Children's Services for a month longer in order to finish his paperwork. The therapist continued working with Lucinda and Kiesha weekly.

Today, Kiesha is five years old and continues living with her mother. Kiesha sings in the children's choir at the church she attends with her mother. Last Christmas, Lucinda invited Mama Brenda and Susan to attend the children's program. Kiesha stood on stage with other children her age, waving wildly to Brenda, Susan, and Lucinda when she saw them in the audience. Lucinda has maintained her sobriety and is working as a treatment coordinator for a drug abuse prevention program.

Happy endings for children like Kiesha don't happen nearly as often as I would like. Looking back over her case and how it evolved, the most critical piece was the relationship work done in therapy, first with her foster mother and then with her biological mother. Parents can complete drug treatment, parenting classes, and counseling successfully without being able or ready to parent their children upon their return. Unless a relationship develops between a parent and a child, and they are supported in being a family unit, chances are good that reunification will not succeed.

Far too often, young children are placed in foster care without any thought given to how they are relating to the adults caring for them. Suppose Kiesha remained in her first foster home and didn't have a therapist working with her. At ages two and three and beyond she might have been a very different child. If the professional team working with Kiesha had not taken care to help her develop healthy attachments, she would have had significant difficulty forming a healthy relationship with Lucinda after Lucinda successfully completed other court-ordered services.

"Up to eighty-two percent of maltreated infants have unhealthy attachments to their caregivers" (Goldsmith, Douglas, Oppenheim, and Wanlass, 2007). While a parent completes reunification services, a baby must be also be given the opportunity to heal from disrupted attachment so that he or she can grow into a healthy, resilient child. Without careful attention to relationship work, babies and parents struggle with each other upon reunification. In worst-case scenarios, young children are reunified with parents only to find themselves back in foster care when it doesn't work.

Because the area of infant mental health is relatively new, there are not many service providers who are skilled and experienced in working with very young children and their caregivers or biological parents. The number of young children entering foster care continues to grow, while the capacity to offer this therapeutic intervention remains limited. Ideally, over time, more clinicians will see the importance of this work and determine that it is extraordinarily rewarding. With the right training and supervision, therapists have the ability to make significant differences in the lives of young children. They have the opportunity to impact not only the current generation, but generations to come.

CHAPTER 10

The Value of Investing

WHEN MARCUS FIESEL WAS removed from his biological mother for the first time, he was just over a year old. He went to foster care for several months until a juvenile court judge returned him to his mother. Would his life have looked different, even been saved, had he and his mother engaged in weekly therapy with a professional determining whether his mother had the capacity to parent him? Would such a therapist have been able to tell the judge that Marcus and his mother struggled in their relationship with one another and his mother was very limited in her ability to take care of him?

When Marcus was placed with the Carrolls, would a therapist have been able to identify the red flags that so many other professionals missed? If Liz and Marcus attended weekly therapy together, would the therapist have been able to glean important information from their interaction and come to the conclusion that he was routinely abused and neglected in the Carrolls' home? Would such therapy sessions have saved his life?

We will never know the answers to these questions. In retrospect, it is easy to say that things should have, and could have, been done differently.

When Marcus came to the attention of child welfare professionals, their response cost the taxpayers money. Federal and state funds paid the salaries of caseworkers who investigated the allegations of child abuse and neglect. Such funds paid the salaries of the magistrate and attorneys who were involved in his juvenile court case. Taxpayers footed the bill for his foster placement and all of the other services he received. Despite these efforts, Marcus is dead. Since Marcus' death, I've thought a lot about his life, his experience on this earth, and what could have saved him. I've thought long and hard, and I've come to the conclusion that his best chance for survival would have cost taxpayers nothing.

Marcus' best chance for survival was in a relationship. A single relationship with any one adult who was able and willing to protect him and care for him, or any one adult with the ability to influence the decisions made about his life. Just one relationship would have had more of an opportunity to save him than all the money and services in the world. Healthy relationships offer a great deal to young children who are getting accustomed to how this world works. Without such relationships, young children have a rough way to go. Reaching troubled babies and toddlers is critical if we wish to keep their problems from growing along with them.

I met Crystal when she was twelve years old and living in a group home for troubled girls. She had lived in dozens of different places by that time, including foster homes, group homes, and residential treatment facilities. I inherited her case from a retiring GAL and when I did, I spent a full day researching the nine volumes of her Children's Services history. The volumes told her life story. Her Children's Services record opened on the day she was born.

The hospital had called Children's Services after Crystal's mother, Tonya, reported she was homeless and using marijuana. Crystal and Tonya tested positive for marijuana at the time of her birth. Children's Services assisted

Tonya in obtaining housing and enrolled her in outpatient drug treatment. Two months later, the caseworker arrived for a home visit and found Crystal and Tonya gone. Tonya had discontinued drug treatment and moved out, taking Crystal with her. It was as if they had vanished. The caseworker closed the case, citing lack of contact with the family as the reason.

They surfaced again when Crystal was eighteen months old. This time, a woman called to report that she had babysat Crystal the night before, and Tonya had not returned to get her. The caller did not know Crystal's mother well, but agreed to keep the toddler because Tonya said she had an emergency and no one else could watch her. Crystal was starving and filthy. She shoveled food into her mouth fist after fist.

A Children's Services caseworker was assigned to investigate the allegation. The investigation revealed that Tonya was a cocaine addict and unwilling to engage in treatment. The caseworker located an uncle who was willing to care for Crystal. After his background checks were completed, and his home was inspected, Crystal went to live with him.

This arrangement lasted only until the caseworker closed the case. As soon as the case closed, Crystal's uncle decided he could no longer take care of her. Crystal then went to live with an adult cousin. This arrangement lasted for six months before she was handed back over to Tonya.

Children's Services became involved again after receiving a call from the police. When the caseworker arrived, Crystal, who was now four, was sitting in the back of a police car. Tonya had approached a stranger and told him she was selling Crystal in exchange for drugs. Name the price, she had said, and she's all yours. Fortunately, the stranger called the police instead. Consequently, Crystal was removed from her mother and placed in foster care.

This time, Tonya entered inpatient drug treatment. As required by law, Tonya was given the opportunity to reunify with her daughter. Tonya was required to complete drug treatment, a psychological evaluation, and parenting classes. Each week, a case-aide drove Crystal from her foster home to the facility where her mother lived in order for the two of them to visit. Crystal had no idea what to make of these weekly visits, and her adjustment back at the foster home took two days. By the time she had finally settled into her routine again, it was time for another visit.

Tonya successfully finished inpatient treatment, and after ninety days, she transitioned to outpatient drug treatment. Crystal's visitation was expanded and changed to unsupervised. They spent the weekends together. Crystal returned to her foster home on Monday mornings, aggressive and full of anger, not to mention hungry. These visits continued for several months. A random urine screen revealed her mother was using cocaine again. Unsupervised visitation ceased and returned to two hours each week, supervised. Soon thereafter, Tonya stopped coming and after several weeks of Crystal being driven to the county agency and waiting in vain for her mother to appear, the court agreed to suspend visitation until Tonya re-engaged in services and committed to consistent visitation. She never followed through.

Crystal was six when her caseworker filed a motion for termination of parental rights. The caseworker believed it was in Crystal's best interest to be made available for adoption. Crystal's GAL was appointed to eighty other children at that time and simply rubber-stamped whatever recommendations the caseworker made.

After two years of court delays and continuances, Crystal was permanently committed to Hamilton County Job and Family Services and made available for adoption. Five more months passed before the caseworker completed the exhaustive paperwork to transfer her case to a new caseworker in the Adoptions Unit, who initiated finding an adoptive home for Crystal.

Crystal was nine years old when she was placed with an adoptive mother and father, along with their two teenage children. Her adoptive family, despite their efforts and good intentions, simply could not manage her. Her temper was uncontrollable, and she exploded into rages on a regular basis. She also was a highly sexualized child. She was ten years old when she engaged in sexual behavior with a four-year-old family friend. Her family sought help for her to no avail. Her adoption failed, and she was back in foster care. She also went through several foster homes. Each time, her placement failed because of her behavior. She lived for a time at a treatment facility for troubled children after she began setting fires. She was kicked out of several schools, once because she threw a chair at the principal.

After advocating for Crystal for two years, I sat around a conference table with a half dozen other social workers, psychiatrists, and psychologists trying to decide how to help her. Nothing seemed to work. She had a number of mental health diagnoses, including Reactive Attachment Disorder, likely stemming from her early life experiences in which she was never able to form a healthy attachment to an adult. I researched and advocated placement for her in the best facilities in our area of the country. No matter where she went for treatment, or what we offered, nothing helped. Her aggression frequently escalated to violence, and even the most skilled and knowledgeable professionals could not help her.

As I sat at that conference table feeling completely helpless in finding solutions to her problems, I couldn't help but wonder what Crystal would look like if one caring, experienced clinician had been involved when she was a year old. If just one caseworker, along with an infant mental health therapist, was monitoring her care and safety and intervening when necessary, would her life be different? If she had remained in the safe arms of a loving adult instead of passed to anyone on the street who would take her, would she have made a better adjustment to her adoptive family? If she had one adult who protected her and nurtured her, would she have had a better shot at growing into a competent adult?

I believe she would have. I believe that if one person had been looking out for her, ensuring her safety, security, growth, and development, she would have had a good chance. It surely would have been a lot easier if we got it right with her the first time, when she was a baby, as opposed to trying to remedy her significant mental health issues and behavior problems later. When Crystal was seventeen, a therapist told me it was useless to try to help anymore. "She's a thug, Holly. Always has been, always will be."

At that precise moment, I decided that because everyone around her had given up, it was even more important that I continue to see only good in her. I continued to advocate for Crystal's best interests in, and out of, court. Despite my best efforts, things never improved for her. On her eighteenth birthday, she walked away from the system. Currently, she is incarcerated for aggravated robbery.

I was Crystal's GAL from the time she was twelve until she turned eighteen. She lived successfully in foster care for only six months of that time. The other five and a half years were spent living in residential treatment facilities in Ohio, Kentucky, and Indiana. Facilities for violent teenagers. For sexual offending teenagers. For teenagers suffering from reactive attachment disorders. We tried a variety of places, hoping something would help. Some of the facilities cost over $300 per day. She lived in those places for months at a time. Sometimes she would progress enough to "step down" to a lower level of care, like an unlocked group home. But then, she would run away, get arrested, and we would start looking for another place to take her.

Although I put everything I had into helping her succeed, the county Children's Services agency was responsible for paying for her treatment. And, the county paid dearly. Over the years, Crystal's placement costs alone topped hundreds of thousands of dollars. Then there was mileage for hundreds of hours-long car rides, the salaries for all the caseworkers who managed her case, and the cost of the salaries of dozens of therapists, psychologists, and psychiatrists. Add the court costs and the salaries of the magistrate, the Children's Services attorney and the endless line of public defenders that represented her each time she was charged with running away. Did her care top a million dollars? I wouldn't be surprised if it did.

Across America, thousands of children like Crystal spend their days in the child welfare system. Child abuse and neglect are not just emotionally devastating for children, although ultimately the children pay the highest price when they are not protected and cared for by the adults in their lives. It can be devastating to taxpayers who provide the financial support that pays for their care. One recent study estimated the annual cost of child abuse and neglect to be $103.8 billion (Wung & Holton, 2007). All the money in the world cannot take away the pain, fear, and anger experienced by children who have been abused and neglected. And unfortunately, investing billions of dollars annually doesn't automatically make life better for those children and families.

Crystal chose to walk away from the system when she turned eighteen. She never explained why, she simply asked to be released. She was living with a friend at the time and was tired, I think, of having system people in her life.

Unfortunately, within months Crystal was back in the system. Not the child welfare system, but the adult criminal system. She was arrested for aggravated robbery. Federal and state dollars will continue to be invested in her care and rehabilitation. Taxpayers will pay for the secured roof over her head and regular meals.

Many incarcerated adults report a history of experiencing abuse or neglect as a child. One study reported as many as 68% of incarcerated adult male felons were abused as children (Weeks & Widom). Another report shows being maltreated in childhood doubles the probability of engaging in many types of crime (Currie, 2006). From this research, we can understand that it makes sense to invest resources in abused and neglected children, particularly when they are young.

Tonight many parents will safely tuck their young children into bed. They will read stories after teeth are brushed and faces are washed. They will turn on nightlights and blow one final kiss as they close the bedroom door, leaving it open just a crack to pacify their precious charges. These parents may stop to whisper a plea for their children to be kept safe throughout their lives.

One of the best ways they can keep them safe is to respond to the plight of abused or neglected children. To think that kids like Crystal are not our problem is simply incorrect. When Crystal pulled a gun on the grocery store clerk, she became his problem. A very big problem.

Crystal had so little experience with kindness and unconditional love that it is not surprising that she had trouble manifesting these in the world. But she shares the world with the rest of us who give our love and kindness freely. This is the world we will leave to our children. Doesn't it make sense to do the very best we can to help all children get off to a good start in life, so that maybe, someday, we will leave the world with an emotionally healthy generation at the helm?

The devastation of Crystal's childhood had significant consequences for her. They weren't lost on me, either. While I couldn't seem to help Crystal, I could learn how to do a better job of understanding infants and toddlers and advocating for them effectively in efforts to help them avoid the kind of life Crystal had.

The fastest growing segment of children coming into foster care is under the age of five. In 2007, nearly 11% of children served by ProKids were under the age of one. By the time they are assigned to ProKids for advocacy, they have been abused, neglected, or abandoned. The world has already been unkind to them in some fashion. I believe it is critical for them to receive infant mental health services. Not because they are mentally ill, but because they have a much better chance of stability and a healthy relationship with an adult if there is a therapist assessing their emotional well-being and working with an adult on how to meet their physical and emotional needs.

If you are ill and go to an emergency room for medical care, you will likely go through triage, where a nurse will ask you questions and make an assessment of what kind of care you need, and the urgency under which it will be given. I have often thought that infants and toddlers coming into foster care would benefit from having an assessment completed regarding their emotional needs and development, along with the adults in their lives.

Imagine how Crystal's life might have turned out if an infant mental health therapist was assigned to her early in her life. Let's say that Crystal and her mother attended weekly sessions with a therapist when Crystal was a newborn, before her mother moved without a forwarding address. Would the therapist have supported the mother enough for her to admit that she just couldn't take care of Crystal?

Several years ago, an infant mental health therapist was working with a mother and her infant daughter. The mother struggled with mental illness and although she was on medication and compliant with services ordered by the court, she simply could not parent her baby. She packed up the baby's things and took her in for their weekly session. Mentally anguished and sobbing, she handed her over to the therapist and told her she could not do it anymore. The therapist worked with her to process this decision and support her. Her baby was placed with a loving family that day and eventually adopted by them. She is thriving. What would her fate have been if her mother did not have a safe, supportive, and non-judgmental place to make her decision?

Crystal was about eighteen months old when her great uncle came forward to take care of her. If Crystal and her great uncle participated in weekly bonding and attachment therapy with an infant mental health therapist, would there have been more information regarding his commitment to take care of her long term? Would red flags have been raised regarding his true intentions and ability to care for her? Would different decisions be made regarding her placement with him if an infant mental health therapist were involved?

Crystal was four when she was placed in foster care and shuttled back and forth between her foster home and weekly visitation with her mother. A therapist was not involved with helping her make sense of her life story and weekly visits. A therapist was not helping the adults in Crystal's life come together to discuss Crystal's experience and how she could best be helped and supported. Would such intervention have reduced the chaos and overwhelming emotion Crystal experienced during this time? Would Crystal be in a better place emotionally to handle these life experiences? How would that have impacted her ability to make healthy relationships with adoptive parents later in her life?

Infant mental health therapists did not exist when Crystal was a baby. But they exist now, and are making a tremendous difference in the lives of young children. However, there are far too few to treat the increasing numbers of infants and toddlers coming into foster care. Additionally, infant mental health is a specialized field. Working with babies and toddlers is much different than working with older children as a traditional therapist. Working with three- and four-year-olds is also very different than working with six- and seven-year-olds.

As a young child, Crystal didn't have a healthy, emotionally nurturing relationship with any one person. She was never able to develop such a relationship as she got older. Healthy relationships continue to elude her as an adult. Far too often, girls like Crystal get pregnant at relatively young ages and begin the cycle of abuse and neglect all over again.

In America today, grandparents are raising increasing numbers of children when their parents have been unable to do so. These children have the best chance at remaining with their siblings, as opposed to being separated in foster care. They also are protected against the trauma of being placed in a home completely unfamiliar to them.

Two siblings, six-year-old Tina, and four-year-old Tyra, were removed from their mother when her drug addiction spiraled out of control. She entered drug treatment, and Tina and Tyra went to live with their grandmother, Mary, who worked full time as a nurse in a doctor's office. Mary was completely committed to Tina and Tyra, and did everything possible to shower them with love and affection and the stability they had not known while they lived with their mother. Mary also lived paycheck to paycheck, like most Americans. She was living in a one-bedroom apartment when the girls came to live with her, prompting her to seek housing with more space to accommodate the three of them.

Tina was enrolled in kindergarten and Tyra spent her days at a childcare center. Tina struggled to keep up with the other children academically, and was barely learning the concepts her teacher was presenting. Her public school offered half day and full day kindergarten and the teacher recommended Tina attend full day. Tina was bright and capable and simply needed the extra time in the classroom in order to make sense of it all. Tina could benefit greatly from all day kindergarten, and the teacher believed that if this occurred, she would have no trouble keeping up with the class when she entered first grade.

Mary was also in favor of all day kindergarten for Tina. Each day Mary had to leave her job at lunchtime to get Tina from school and take her to the childcare center. Tina arrived at the center just in time for lunch and her afternoon nap, though she had not napped in several years. She wanted to be in school all day with the other kids.

Unfortunately, Mary could not afford the $250 each month for all day kindergarten class. She couldn't piece together enough money each month to make ends meet with this additional cost. Ohio law does not require full day kindergarten, therefore families must pay tuition if they choose full day as opposed to half day.

The school year passed with Mary racing to get Tina every day on her lunch hour, and then racing back to her office for afternoon patients. Mary often had to stay late and finish work she couldn't get to because of her long lunch hour. At the end of each day, she raced to reach the childcare center before it closed at 6 p.m.

The ProKids CASA assigned to advocate for Tina and Tyra in court spent lots of time researching different ways to get full day kindergarten funded. She talked to everyone from the county caseworker to the school superintendent. Her efforts were unsuccessful, and in the end, Tina stayed in the half-day class, barely passing on to first grade.

As the CASA and I discussed this issue and brainstormed together about ways to get the funding, I couldn't help but think back to Crystal. Federal and state money covered several hundred dollars per day for her placement in residential treatment facilities, but there was no money for full day kindergarten for a child who had experienced abuse and neglect and was in danger of falling behind academically. That's not to say that we should not have done everything we could to help Crystal as a teenager. Of course, we should have, and we did. But it makes just as much sense to give children like Tina a better start in school if it is available.

Recently, significant findings have been made as a result of research into brain development. Scientific evidence has proven that the first three years of life are the most critical developmental period of life. Early life experiences shape the way children grow physically, emotionally, and cognitively.

To that end, programs have been developed across the nation to support and nurture the growth of young children at risk of abuse and neglect. Many of these programs include a home visitation component. At-risk young children and their families are visited by a nurse or social worker who supports and educates parents regarding the needs of their children and how to best help them grow physically and emotionally. "Home visitation programs have been shown to reduce juvenile delinquency by reducing abuse and neglect, thereby reducing the likelihood that these potential victims of violence may one day engage in criminal behavior or become violent offenders" (Child Welfare League of America, 2006). In short, the more we do to help up front, the better off these children are. Our entire society benefits long term as well.

Unfortunately, young children who have already experienced abuse or neglect are rarely able to benefit from this type of intervention. When I began the Building Blocks program at ProKids in 2000, it was largely because young foster children were unable to benefit from a newly unveiled home visitation program designed to target at-risk young children. By the time they came into foster care, they were no longer considered at-risk. The damage had already occurred, and now the child welfare system was responsible for helping families rectify the problems they faced. The problem with this logic is that risk of abuse and neglect does not automatically stop for children once they are placed in foster care.

We may be tempted to avoid a child's placement in foster care at all costs, reasoning that such placement is a known trauma to a child. It is traumatic to lose everything you know including your home, your parents, your school, and sometimes your siblings. Fear of the unknown is often greater that fear of the known. But we cannot, and should not, avoid foster care when 27.4% of child deaths are at the hands of their biological parents (U.S. Department of Health and Human Services, 2006). Foster care is necessary and life saving.

When I read the daily newspaper, stories relating to abused and neglected children seem to jump off the page. I'm immediately drawn to them, skipping articles relating to the issue of the day, whether it is government spending, or political matters. I barely notice the weather or the advice column. I want to know what is going on in my hometown when it comes to children.

One day several months after Marcus Fiesel's death, there were two articles in the paper related to child abuse and neglect and foster care. One story was about a mother who brutally killed her infant. The story mentioned that Children's Services had been involved with the family, but that the baby had not been removed from the mother. Further into the newspaper, an article discussed the problems of the foster care system. It's no wonder caseworkers are buried under the pressure of life and death situations, knowing that a mistake could cost a child's life and land them on the front page of the daily news.

It's also no wonder that newspaper readers throw their hands up and choose to look the other way. How can a member of the general community feel empowered to impact change in such a difficult system? We know biological parents sometimes choose to beat, starve, and abandon their children.

We also know that foster parents sometimes do the same things. In a wash of helplessness, it is easy to look the other way.

Just yesterday, I was entering the courthouse on my way to a hearing regarding infant twins who had been abandoned. As I approached the courthouse doors, I found myself walking alongside a county caseworker. She has been a caseworker for years and we have worked together in the past. We said our hellos and asked each other how it was going. She is a mother of four children who are nearly the same ages as my three. We flashed our badges to the security guard and pushed the elevator button. As we caught up with each other, I asked her why we choose to do the job we do. It would be easier to live in suburban America and isolate ourselves from the troubles abused and neglected children face. How simple it would be to put on our blinders and never see these children who share our community.

Her answer was simple and profound. "We do it," she said, "because when we see these helpless children staring up at us, we see how much they need us. How can we not do it?"

Even though some adults perpetuate abuse and neglect on children, most adults do not. Although some adults are unable to look beyond their own immediate needs, most adults instinctively put children first. Although some adults work daily to support and save children who are lost in the system, most adults don't realize they exist.

Marcus Fiesel changed all that. Bound by tape and put in a closet, completely helpless, he made a powerful impact on the communities surrounding where he lived. He removed the blinders most of us had on. Little Marcus put a face on all of the invisible foster children, putting their needs front and center. It is virtually impossible to look at a picture of him, his blue eyes blazing in the golden sun, fields of green behind him, and then to not see the burdens facing children like him who are left behind.

While Liz and David Carroll went to prison for his death, their girl-friend, Amy Baker, did not. Amy was the prosecution's star witness against the Carrolls and was offered immunity because she had not directly harmed Marcus. Many people were outraged. The public made constant demands that she be punished for her role in his death, including helping David burn, then later dump, his remains. People wanted justice for Marcus, and they were looking to the criminal court system to provide it.

I believe that justice for Marcus lies in our commitment to help the foster children who are still here, living among us and sharing schools, parks, and playgrounds with our children. Which honors Marcus and his suffering more, our anger or our promise to do better by all children? His story can bring out the best in you now. Your actions can help save these children who need you. You have the power to create goodness from the ashes of Marcus' death.

CHAPTER 11

Marcus' Legacy

BEFORE MARCUS FIESEL, I felt like I worked in a shadow world. Foster children took the backseat to many other societal issues such as the care of our environment, politics, and the economy. After Marcus, foster care was front and center in the local media and in the hearts and minds of ordinary people.

Marcus' death was common knowledge for only a few days when I headed to my office one morning. I had a little extra time after getting my own children off to school, and I decided to treat myself to a latte from a local coffee shop on my way to work. My heart was heavy and I almost dreaded another day of dealing with the aftermath of Marcus' case. I was feeling devastation at what he had endured, helplessness at what could be done for the remainder of these precious children, and frustration at a system so clearly broken. I needed all the help I could get. A latte couldn't undo all that, but it would be a small gift to myself in the midst of a difficult day.

As soon as I opened the door to the coffee shop, I felt it. I stood for a moment and surveyed the scene around me. Fellow coffee drinkers sat with their morning java, pouring over the local newspaper, the inside pages open to a spread of pictures of Marcus along with the details of his short life. Some wiped tears from their eyes as they read. Others read with a look of disbelief on their faces, color draining from them while they ingested the details along with their coffee. I caught snippets of people's conversations as the coffee grinders wailed in the background. "Can you believe it?"

"How could someone do something so horrific?"

"Foster parents are only in it for the money."

"Every child living in a Lifeway foster home should be taken away. Those people can't be trusted."

"Caseworkers are lazy and incompetent. How could they not see what was happening in Marcus' foster home?"

"Where is the government in all of this? How could they let this happen?"

I waited in line. Their emotions poured over me as my coffee was prepared. I thought of Adam's and Sarah's foster parents, whose embraces were strong, yet gentle enough to diminish Adam's and Sarah's grief and pain. I thought of two-year-old Colin, whose Lifeway foster parents transformed him from a malnourished, failure-to-thrive infant into a robust, happy toddler. I thought of caseworkers who worked fourteen-hour days and left voice mail messages for me at 2 a.m. I thought of magistrates who asked so many questions that, sometimes, it overwhelmed me.

I resisted the urge to pull up a chair and join these conversations. I wanted to answer the questions about how the government could let this happen. Parenting well is a task we struggle with in our own families every day. Did we really think the government would parent these vulnerable children with any success? If easy answers existed within the system, we would have found them by now.

The reality is that the answers don't exist in the system. They exist in each of us. The beauty of our diversity is that we all excel at something. We all have something to offer the world and to these children who need us. We can't all do everything, but we can all do something. Our involvement in issues related to foster children is more critical now than even three years ago. The landscape of child welfare has changed dramatically since 2006 when Marcus died at the hands of his foster parents. Due to the downturn in our economy, it is worse.

Today, the government system charged with overseeing the care of foster children faces crippling budget cuts due to our current economic crisis. There are fewer foster homes in Hamilton County to meet the needs of children who cannot be maintained with biological families for reasons of abuse or neglect. Due to layoffs at Children's Services agencies across the nation, there is less supervision of caseworkers and fewer support staff. In Hamilton County, there is no money left for relatives who step up to care for children whose parents have failed them. Adoptions subsidies are reduced, and post-adoption services for children have been eliminated. All of this is happening at a time when child abuse cases are more heinous than ever, a record number of people are coming to Job and Family Services for help, and incidents of domestic violence are soaring. Children are often caught in the crossfire.

What does this mean for foster children? It means they are less likely to find safety, stability, and nurturing in families that love them. Day by day they lose a piece of their childhood until there is nothing left. It doesn't have to be this way. Together, we can prevent this from happening. It's time for us to pay attention to the little ones whose lives are left in tattered shreds, depending on a government system in crisis to save them. The help is not coming. We must step into this mess and be the help these children are desperately waiting for.

Not too long ago, I spent a Saturday afternoon at a soccer field while each of my three children played their favorite sport. The weather was beautiful. The sky was a brilliant shade of blue, and the hot summer days had melted into cool breezes. The leaves of several large trees showed off their first shades of golden yellow. It was the perfect backdrop to the kids running around outside as they waited for games to begin or their sibling's games to end. While I enjoyed watching my kids play, I also enjoyed catching up with all the other parents whom I hadn't seen all summer. I liked seeing how their kids had grown and hearing how school was going. I sat back and watched the dads double-knot shoelaces and kick a ball with their kids. For a little while, the world of foster children faded. Until my cell phone rang.

It was a CASA, Olivia, calling me about her case. Demarco, age two, and his brother, Leonard, age ten months, had been living with their grandparents. Children's Services took emergency custody of the boys six months earlier. Anita, their biological mother, refused to leave her boyfriend. Shawn was a registered sex offender. The police had been called four times to Anita's apartment and had charged Shawn with domestic violence. Court orders forbade Shawn to be around Anita or the children. Despite that, Anita and Shawn continued their relationship. Consequently, Demarco and Leonard were placed in a foster home for three weeks and then moved to the home of their grandparents, who had come forward to take them. The grandparents knew that Anita was not permitted to have unsupervised contact with the children. The court ordered all contact between the children and Anita to be supervised by Children's Services. The grandparents agreed, and assured the magistrate, and the rest of us, that they would not allow Anita to be with her children alone.

Olivia was beside herself. The night before, police had responded to a 911 call from Anita's neighbor. The caller reported hearing glass breaking and heavy objects being thrown amidst a woman's screams. The police responded and found Anita with a busted lip and Shawn with gashes up and down his arms. They had also found Demarco and Leonard hiding under the kitchen table. Leonard was curled up in a fetal position with Demarco's little arms trying to hold him protectively. Anita's grandparents had been allowing Anita to take the kids on the weekends, assuming no one would find out that they were violating court orders on a Saturday and Sunday.

Demarco and Leonard were placed in an emergency foster home at 3 a.m., wearing only t-shirts and diapers. No clothes or shoes, much less any information about the formula Leonard was on or the fact that Demarco was allergic to peanuts. Olivia relayed the horror story, but didn't feel a sense of relief that the children were safely in foster care. She was worried even more. Their prior foster parents did not have space available in their home, so Demarco and Leonard were forced into another unfamiliar environment. In the scramble to find a foster home for the boys, they were placed in the only home available. These foster parents could only keep Demarco and Leonard for three days and were angry that the children had come to them sick. Both of the boys were running fevers and had diarrhea. They would need to be moved again for the fourth time in six months.

I had walked away from the families around me to take Olivia's call. After we talked for a while, Olivia had her to do list compiled. Her tasks included visiting the boys the next day, passing on all information about Leonard's formula and feeding routines as well as Demarco's allergies. Over the next week, she would work with the caseworker and make arrangements to get all of the boys' things from their grandparents' home. She and the caseworker would also work to find a more suitable placement for the boys, preferably a local foster home where they could be together, and one in which the foster parents would be willing to participate in therapy with the boys as they began to heal from their trauma. It was a tall order, but Olivia was determined to succeed. The boys' caseworker was phenomenal, and she and Olivia worked well as a team. I knew together they would find a way.

I finished our phone call and returned to families milling about the park on a beautiful fall day. Gail, whose daughter plays with my own, had joined them. Gail held a leash attached to a darling black and brown dog. He was a friendly little pup, thrilled to be outside, soaking up the day and all the activity. He happily sniffed everything he could, and promptly stretched out on the ground at the first hint of a hand to pet his belly. I couldn't resist the outstretched belly and wagging tail, and Gail and I talked while I petted her little friend.

"He's so darling, Gail. I didn't know you were getting another dog."

"We hadn't planned on it, but Sammy, our yellow lab really needs some companionship during the day and we thought adding another dog to the household would be good for her."

"How's it working out with the two of them?" I asked.

"So far so good. We took Sammy to the dog pound to meet her several times and they did OK with each other. We only have her on a weekend visit to see how it goes. It's going pretty well, so I think on Monday morning we'll call the pound and let them know we'd like to keep her."

It made a lot of sense to thoughtfully add an animal to the family in steps. Three meetings. A weekend visit. It's ideal, really.

If only Demarco and Leonard had a chance to be thoughtfully transitioned into a new home. If only there were families lined up to take children in the middle of the night, no matter what crisis precipitated the placement. If only we had homes where Demarco and Leonard could belong not only to a family, but also to a larger community committed to giving them safety, stability, and a lot of love and nurturing. Wouldn't it be wonderful if these two little boys could be absorbed by a family dedicated to helping them heal and grow, surrounded by a community that supports them all?

I don't have any doubt that if I told Gail and the others about Demarco and Leonard, they would have done anything they could to help these little boys. Gail and millions like her would respond to a child in need, if only they knew what to do to help.

Contrasting Demarco and Leonard's life experience with those of my own children and the children of moms like Gail left me sleepless that night. Questions grabbed hold of my mind and would not let go. Why do some children have one or two parents who meet their every need with attentiveness while some children don't have a single adult in the world to protect them? Why are some children showered with love and affection and other children starved for a kind word? Why is it that two children who live in the same country, the same town, the same neighborhood, and sometimes even the same house are treated so differently? Why is life kind to some and harsh to others?

These are questions I couldn't answer then, and I haven't answered them since. I've come to accept that the answers will elude me in this lifetime. Perhaps I will find them in the next. However, I did come to one conclusion. I was looking for answers to the wrong questions. The question is not, "Why is it this way?" Instead, the question is, "Given it is this way, what do I do?" What is my part in all of this? While I can't save children like Demarco and Leonard from abuse or neglect, I can certainly do something. What is it?

These are the kinds of questions that adults in Marcus' community struggled with after his death. In the weeks following his death, potential volunteers streamed through the doors at the ProKids office, learning more about children in foster care and how they could be helped. They brought their questions and horror over Marcus along with a commitment to do something. One by one, newly trained CASA volunteers joined ProKids in their quest to ensure safe, permanent, and nurturing homes for children. In the fall months of 2005, one year prior to Marcus, eighteen community members contacted ProKids to learn more about how they could become a part of the solution to the problems facing abused and neglected children (ProKids, 2005). In the fall of 2006 following Marcus, this number jumped to fifty-six (ProKids, 2006).

This sudden increase in volunteers renewed hope that somehow good could be brought from Marcus' horrible death. There are countless ways to help the invisible foster kids living in every community across our nation. Some require a commitment of time, some require a commitment of money, and some will take a piece of your heart. All can be life changing for children who are waiting for the world to take care of them.

A Dozen Ways to Make a Difference

1. **Pay attention and spend some time researching child abuse.** As you read the newspaper and watch the news, pay close attention to the stories relating to children who have been beaten, raped, or who are otherwise victims of violent crimes. Know that their trauma and suffering do not automatically end once authorities step in. Their healing depends on the nurturing and competence of the adults left in charge of their care. Being aware that these children exist is the first step in accepting that they are within your midst, living in your communities. Once you realize they are close, you are one step closer to active involvement.

    When I began writing this book, I knew my writing would come largely from my experience. However, when I turned to the research regarding abuse and neglect, I was amazed at how much information was at my fingertips. Countless studies have been conducted and briefs written on best-practices for child welfare systems. Judges, psychologists, and other talented professionals have spent a lot of time and energy in figuring out what works for foster kids. Why then, I wondered, do so many children continue to suffer, to fall through the cracks in the system? Then it dawned on me. It is because the communities of average citizens surrounding these children haven't been invited to be active participants in these issues. They haven't been tapped to share their resources of time, talent, and treasure. Take time to read up on some of the recommendations and findings made. Some good websites to visit are www.cwla.org (Child Welfare League of America) and www.pewfostercare.org (Pew Commission on Children in Foster Care).

2. **Learn about the political process, how it influences decisions about abused and neglected children, and where the government dollars funneled to supporting programs and agencies go. Use this knowledge, along with your political voice, to vote for politicians who support funding and the development of programs for abused and neglected children.** There is no more important function our government takes on our behalf than actions to care for abused, neglected, and dependent children. Most people know very little about what happens to these children once they are placed in foster care or how decisions are made on their behalf. Until masses of people know more, they cannot form communities around these children to impact change.

Engage yourself in the political process and realize that you are the voice of children who do not have one of their own. When public school districts have a levy on the ballot, hundreds of parents, teachers, school administrators and community leaders come together to support the levy and work very hard to get it passed. The greater the involvement and commitment of ordinary citizens, the greater the likelihood it will pass. Think about how foster children have no ability to come together and initiate change or advocate for themselves. We must join together and do it for them. It is the only way they will ever have a collective voice.

Powerful networks dedicated to advocating for children are desperately in need of your interest and support. Voices for America's Children is such a network dedicated to speaking up for children in all forms of government. As a concerned and active community member, you can become the bridge between what happens in federal, state and local governments and the children on the frontline of child abuse. Visit www.voices.org for more information.

3. **Organize events to benefit foster children.** Recently a brownie troop held a book drive, with all proceeds going to ProKids. This little group raised $350 in one day, and in turn, bought gift cards for groceries, gas, and super-stores. These gift cards were used to support grandparents and other relatives raising children on fixed incomes. Some very generous children have chosen to forgo birthday presents in lieu of donations of back-to-school supplies or other necessities for foster children. Extraordinarily talented quilters, through Project Linus, donated exquisite quilts and blankets for ProKids Building Blocks Program, so that when we conduct our first home visits we have something special for the children, made with love. In Hamilton County, the Foster Care Enrichment Council exists to fund things that government dollars cannot cover, such as college application fees. Neediest Kids of All relies entirely upon donations from community members, and they fund summer camps, extra-curricular activities and other programs that are important for a foster child to experience. During the holiday season, a number of churches or schools adopt our children or families and buy gifts. Lawyers from the Cincinnati Bar Association have been doing this for many years.

4. **Give your money or your time.** Every non-profit serving foster children relies on the generosity of donors. At ProKids, we could not impact the lives of so many children without the financial support of many grants, foundations, and individual donors. Every non-profit, even those with a large volunteer base, has electricity bills to pay and computer systems to maintain. In this economy, non-profits are hurting just as much, if not more, than larger corporations who are forced to do more with less. Non-profits agencies forced to do more with less may mean the difference between saving a child or not.

    No money? Just lost your job and looking for work? If so, this is a perfect time to volunteer. One unexpected by-product of service to others is the great satisfaction we get from knowing we made a difference in the life of a child. Volunteering can give us valuable new perspectives and bring new friends into our lives. Contact your local United Way to find a list of non-profit agencies that need your help.

5. **Make it a family affair.** Not too long ago a sixth grade teacher at a private school asked me to come and talk to her class about how they could help foster children. I agreed, albeit slightly reluctantly. I wasn't sure how twelve-year-olds could really help, and I didn't want to overwhelm them with the realities of foster care. However, it turned out to be a wonderful experience. A month later, I received thank you letters from the students. Their comments were eye-opening and inspiring. "My family prays for foster children every night now." "When I grow up, I think I would like to have a job where I can help these kids." "My parents are talking about fostering and I think it would be good for us to share our home with a child who needs a family." Someday, these children will step into their futures and leadership roles. How wonderful it would be if we nurtured their hearts to care for the vulnerable, lost, and forgotten.

6. **Volunteer at a local school.** Many parents today don't have the luxury of volunteering at their child's school. They are working to put food on the table. I'll never forget a ProKids CASA who was assigned to a second grade boy. Over eighty percent of the students in his school qualified for the free and reduced lunch program. She went to the school to meet his teacher and see how he was progressing. In her discussion with the teacher, she learned that there were no parents willing or able to be a "homeroom mother," whose responsibilities included planning holiday parties. The CASA signed up for the job. Imagine the kids' delight when she appeared for the Thanksgiving Day Party dressed as a giant turkey, complete with games and treats.

Many foster children are behind their peers academically. Oftentimes they change schools midway through the year due to changes in foster home placements. Tutoring a foster child is a valuable service and can make a huge difference in a child's ability to succeed academically. A volunteer tutor may be the only adult that offers consistency in a child's educational experience.

7. **Offer your professional services to help a foster child.** I envision a day when each county has a list of volunteers who offer to do pro bono work for foster children. Are you a hairdresser willing to help a foster kid? There are hundreds of teen girls in foster care with no one to treat them to a salon makeover. Are you a dentist? Dental emergencies for children in foster care are a nightmare. Finding treatment in a timely manner is nearly impossible. Keep in mind that direct contact with foster children will require background checks.

I have called upon the services of many people to help in very specific ways. My sister, who is a pharmacist, answers all my questions about medications prescribed for children and researches them fully. She provides a detailed list of uses, side effects and concerns to consider. An eye doctor examined a foster child for free when there was no way to get him into a clinic within three months.

If volunteering directly to help a foster child does not appeal to you, remember that non-profit agencies serving foster children can also benefit from the gift of your talent and expertise. A wonderful, skilled computer consultant volunteers his time to assist ProKids in managing our computer systems. A Public Relations/Marketing Expert donates her services to help spread the word about the important work done by CASAs. There are endless ways to make your own unique contribution.

8. **Mentor a teen in foster care.** In 2006, nearly 25,000 teens aged out of foster care and entered into adulthood, many of them ill-prepared to meet the challenges of independence. Very few of these young adults have any kind of safety net or community support to fall back on. They are suddenly thrust into adulthood, responsible for their education or employment, managing their money, maintaining a place to live and dealing with a million other details most of us had no idea how to handle when we were 18. Who do they call when the electricity goes out? When they don't know how to fill out paperwork for college applications or government assistance? Who helps them file their taxes, get their driver's license, or helps them shop for a car when they have finally saved enough money? Who remembers their birthday, or the anniversary of the day their mother or father left them at the doorstep of the county agency because they couldn't care for them? Who checks in on them when they have the flu, and who drives them to the doctor when they are too sick to get there alone? These kids desperately need mentors and community around them if they have any real chance of being successful. When a former foster child who "made it" tells his or her story, there is usually

one common theme that runs through all of them. That common theme is the fact that they had someone to count on. You can be that someone for a child who is trying to make it alone.

9. **Encourage your place of worship to get involved in foster care and adoption and support foster parents who have opened their hearts and homes to children.** Across the country, churches seem to be awakening to the plight of children in foster care. Rick Warren, Pastor of Saddleback Church in California and author of *The Purpose Driven Life*, is helping spearhead efforts to reach out to foster children. A foster or adoptive family supported and encouraged by an entire congregation gives a child a place in a home as well as in a community of people who care for them. In Chapter Three you met Thomas, who was five-months-old when he had to leave his foster home because his foster father had a major heart attack and the family was absorbed in that crisis. If his foster family had a solid base of community support, could they have kept him? If they had friends who could babysit, make meals and otherwise support this family unit, would Thomas have avoided a change in placement? Building community around foster children is critical in stabilizing them and helping them heal.

In Cincinnati, Ohio, Every Child's Hope International was formed to motivate and mobilize the church and community to look after the orphans, the children in foster care, and all hungry, thirsty, and abandoned children. A group of 28 churches in Greater Cincinnati came together to join forces and improve the lives of foster children by supporting and encouraging fostering, adopting, and educating the larger community on how these children can be served. For more information, visit www. coalitionofcare.org.

In 2007, Lifesprings, a Cincinnati church, invited foster mothers to join other women for an evening of pampering. This invitation was a huge lift to foster mothers who rarely take time to do something nice for themselves and they felt validated and appreciated for the difficult job they do. It was powerful to witness women coming together to support each other and have a good time.

After the death of Marcus, foster parents faced a lot of hostility from people who felt overwhelmed with the story of Marcus' death and lashed out at foster parents in general, wrongly drawing conclusions that all of them were fostering for the wrong reasons. It has been a trying time for foster parents devoted to children and to giving them everything they can to help them have a safe and happy childhood. If you know foster parents who are working hard at saving children, thank them for their efforts and do something nice for their family. The simple gift of items like movie passes go a long way in making a foster family feel appreciated.

A good friend of mine recently became a foster parent for the first time to a thirteen-month-old little girl who was brought to her home at 9 p.m. with just a t-shirt and diaper. By the next morning, a neighbor had left a case of diapers and some board books along with a nice note thanking my friend for saying yes to a baby who needed her. The next day, more friends brought clothes and toys and a special baby blanket. Over the next several weeks, gifts and items for the baby arrived frequently. By the time the county caseworker issued a voucher for clothes, my friend was able to hand it back. She asked the caseworker to keep it and pass it along to another family who really needed it. This kind of action saves the county financial resources and allows the community to step in and do just a little for a child in need.

10. **Become a Court Appointed Special Advocate (CASA).** Volunteering as a CASA puts you in the position of helping influence critical issues relating to a child. A CASA is a courtroom presence, where life and death decisions are made every day. CASAs are the people who go to great lengths to serve a child. They are adults who have the time to learn every detail of a child's life, right down to a child's favorite color or subject in school. It is a volunteer opportunity that is intense and challenging, but among the most rewarding life experiences you may ever have. Visit www.prokids.org or www.nationalcasa.org for more information.

11. **Become a foster parent.** I have a tremendous amount of respect for people who take hurt children into their homes and love them as their own, while knowing that at any moment they may be forced to say good-bye. It takes a great heart to provide comfort, safety and love for a child who has never experienced such. I once complimented a wonderful foster parent on how much she had changed the course of a little girl's life. I mentioned that I didn't know if I could do it. It would be so hard to love a child as my own knowing she could be taken from me at any moment. The foster mother replied that she was an adult and could shoulder the emotional burdens of fostering. She couldn't turn her back on children because of the pain it may cause her. Devoted foster parents change the lives of children. It is amazing to see children transformed under the loving care of foster parents. Within a week of placement, they visibly look different. They come alive. Color bursts from their cheeks. It is nothing short of miraculous.

12. **Become a forever family for a child who desperately needs one.** Adoption is the ultimate gift people can give a child who does not belong to a family. Adoptive parents put their hearts on the line to give children a chance at a childhood. There are thousands of children awaiting adop-

tion in our country. Without adoptive parents, a child will languish in the system and transition into adulthood without support.

If these suggestions are not something you can do right now, you can still do something. Commit to practicing one act of kindness. Such acts are very powerful, and you can never fully know the impact you may have, particularly when you reach out to a stranger expecting nothing in return.

When my two oldest girls were born eighteen months apart, life was hectic. In fact, when our second daughter, Grace, was born, our baby announcement read, "Look who joined our funny farm." My husband and I were running on empty all the time, while working so hard to be the very best mom and dad we could be. When I was out in public with the girls, strangers would occasionally remark how lovely and happy they both appeared to be. These comments usually came at the time when I needed them the most. I needed to be reminded that I was doing OK as a mom, and that my girls were fine, despite the many mistakes Ed and I made. I was so grateful for the words of kindness or encouragement that I received from strangers. It made the world feel smaller and safer, and as if everything was going to be just fine.

Mindful of the power of those simple comments, I often try to pass them forward. When I go to court for hearings, I usually share the elevator ride up with young mothers toting infants and toddlers with them. As often as I can, I compliment a mother. I notice how well cared for a child looks, or how pleasant and content, and tell his or her mom what a good job she must be doing. On occasion, a mother will break into a wide smile. For a moment, she is transformed by a simple kind word. I can't help but believe she will pass that good feeling onto her baby.

Marcus' community was captivated by his alleged disappearance in the park. In his disappearance and death, he became the community's child. The community responded as though he was one of their own. People searched for him, prayed for him, and wept as they learned of his horrific death. Marcus moved his community in ways no child ever had. Marcus became one of our own. What we didn't realize was that he always had been. Now that we realize children like him drift through our communities without being seen, it is time to open our eyes to the realization that we can and must help them.

During the four years I spent as a Children's Services caseworker, I witnessed horrendous suffering. I became a regular fixture in poverty-stricken neighborhoods as I checked on at-risk children. I accompanied police to pry toddlers from their drug-addicted mothers and place them in foster care, my own pregnant belly hampering my ability to carry a baby out the door to the safety of my car, while police with guns drawn arrested her parents. My arms tried to absorb the pain of a sobbing six-year-old girl who begged me to take her home and be her mother. I said many prayers during this time, for my safety, for the broken children, and for their parents who just couldn't get it together.

As a Guardian Ad Litem, I've introduced myself to, and shaken hands with, fathers who have raped their young daughters and mothers who left their children living in filth while they hit the town for days at a time. Even after all of this, I still firmly believe in the good of humanity. When Marcus was reported missing, two thousand people turned out to search for him. Two thousand. Why did so many abandon their afternoon plans to go search for a little boy?

I believe they did it because people are fundamentally good at heart. When they know what to do to help, they respond. When they are asked to complete a specific duty to assist someone and they are capable of doing it, they will. Just look at the outpouring of support for people whose homes and lives are devastated by floods, fires, or tornados. After 9/11, people all over

U.S. General Accounting Office. (1995).

US General Accounting Office. (2003). GAO-03-357. www.cwla.org/advo-cacy/nationalfactsheet06.htm.

U.S. Department of Health and Human Services. (2001). AFCARS report.

U.S. Dept. of Health and Human Services. (2002). Child Maltreatment Administration on Children, Youth and Families.

US Department of Health and Human Services. (2006). Child Maltreatment Figure 4.2.

Weeks, R. & Widom, C., Ph.D. *National institute of justice report. Self reports of early childhood victimization among incarcerated male felons.*

Wulczyn, E., & Hislop, K. (2002). Babies in foster care: The numbers call for attention.

Zero to Three Journal, 22 (4), 14-15.

Wung, Chink Tung & Holton, John. (2007). Prevent child abuse America: Total estimated cost of child abuse and neglect in the United States. Economic Impact Study.

Youcha, Victoria. Research summary: Children exposed to violence. *Zero to Three Journal.*

Zero to Three Journal. (2001, April/May). 5.

Zero to Three/National Center for Clinical Infant Programs. (1994).

Zimmerman, Julie Irwin. (2007). *Cincinnati Magazine.*

WEB SITES

www.aypf.org/forumbriefs/2006/fb021006.htm.

www.luminafoundation.org.

www.luminafoundation.org/research/what_we_know/index.html#dimension1.

If you'd like to invite Holly Schlaack to speak to your group,
or for information on bulk book sales,
please visit www.invisiblekidsthebook.com.

the country responded to the tragedy by sending bottled water and other necessary items to New York City. After Hurricane Katrina, US citizens traveled to the devastated area to deliver supplies and assist with the cleanup. Several years later, organized groups of volunteers still return to New Orleans to rebuild homes and churches. Many people donate money for these and other causes. When we are called to help, most of us do.

In the world today, it is very easy to feel small and insignificant. There are a great many problems facing countries around the world. Tens of thousands of people die in violent earthquakes or other natural disasters. I feel powerless when I see such overwhelming numbers dominate the world news. I cannot begin to grasp the severity of what is unfolding around the globe.

I suggest that we start small, improving our communities by taking better care of the children who share them with us. When we do, we become part of something that is bigger than we are. It connects us to others in a very powerful way. This in turn leads to positive feelings. And who among us couldn't use a few more of those in our everyday lives?

Stephen Post, author and President of the Institute for Research on Unlimited Love, Altruism, Compassion and Service, has spent years studying the topic of service. "When we give of ourselves, especially if we are young, everything from self-realization to physical health is significantly affected. Mortality is delayed. Depression is reduced. Well-being and good fortune are increased" (Post). Do we need any better reasons than these to commit today to improve the lives of foster children? It is good for us. It is good for them. It is good for entire communities.

Foster children don't have the choices we have. They don't choose their foster parents, their schools, or whether they will get to live with their brothers and sisters. They don't choose the home where they will reside, the caseworker who monitors their care, or the judge who will make life-changing decisions on their behalf. They don't get to choose where they will grow up or who will love them. They live each day at the mercy of a system that sometimes works and sometimes fails. They have no idea day to day which part of the system they will see: the good or the bad.

We, however, have an abundance of choices before us each morning when we awake. Most of us get to choose where we will live, whom we will marry, and how we will raise our family. We get to choose whether we have relationships with a variety of people, whether they are our adult siblings, our neighbors, or the parents of our children's friends. We get to choose the kind of career we will have, if we want one, and how we will leave our mark on this world.

We also choose what to do with the information we have about foster children and the vulnerabilities they face. We can choose to continue looking the other way, or we can choose to do something to help. We can choose to believe that justice for Marcus was achieved in a criminal court, his foster parents spending years in jail paying for their crimes. Or we can find justice for Marcus in our commitment to saving children like him, children who will wake up today, not knowing where they belong or who will love them. We can choose to remain focused solely on our own children and those close to us, or we can choose to help the young foster children who will share this world and the future with our own children.

The choice is yours.

www.invisiblekidsthebook.com

REFERENCES

Bruner, C., Goldbert, J., & Kot, V. (1999). *The ABC's of early childhood: Trends, information and evidence for use in developing an early childhood system of care and education.*

Bruner, C., Goldbert, J., & Kot, V. (2004, Spring). *Juvenile and Family Court Journal*, 55, No. 2, 16.

Cincinnati Enquirer. (2006, September 3). Short, sad life of Marcus Fiesel.

Cohen and Youcha. (2004, Spring). Zero to three: Critical issues for the juvenile and family court. *Juvenile and Family Court Journal.* 55 (2). 15.

Cohen, Julie & Youcha, Victoria. (2004, Spring). Zero to three: Critical issues for the juvenile and family court. *Juvenile and Family Court Journal*, 55 (2). 16-17.

Coolidge, S. (2006, August 29). Marcus left in closet, burned. *Cincinnati Enquirer.*

Coolidge, S. (2007, April 25). Foster Homes A Safe Haven? *Cincinnati Enquirer.*

Courtncy et al. (2005). *Midwest evaluation of the adult functioning of former foster youth: outcomes at age 19.* Chapin Hall.

Currie, Janet. (2006, April). *Does child abuse cause crime?* Columbia University.

Child Welfare League of America. (2006, September). Testimony on home visitation programs.

Dicker, S. & Gordon, E. (2002, April/May). The story of the healthy development checklist for children in foster care. *Zero to Three Journal*, 22 (5), 28.

Federal Medicaid Law. 42 U.S.C. Section 1396(a) (10) and (43) (2000); 42 U.S.C. Section 1396d (a) (4) (B) (2000) and 1396 (r).

Fonargy, P. (2001). *Attachment theory and psychoanalysis.* New York: Other Press.

Foster care adoption fact sheet. Dave Thomas Foundation. www.DaveThomas FoundationforAdoption.org.

Hawley, Theresa, PhD. (2000). *Starting smart.*

Goldsmith, D., Oppenheim, D. & Wanlass, J. (2004). Separation and reunification: Using attachment theory and research to inform decisions affecting placements of children in foster care. *Juvenile and Family Court Journal*, 55(2), 2.

Justice for Marcus. Local12.com, Special Section.

Koenen, Karestan C., Moffitt, Terrie E., Caspi, Avshalom, Taylor, Allan & Purcell. (2003). Development and Psychopathology. 15(2003). 297-311. Cambridge University Press.

Maier, Timothy W. (1997*). Suffer the children.* National Foster Care Education Project. Insight on the News.

Nash, Madeleine. (1997, February). Fertile minds. *Time Magazine*, 149 no. 5, 2.

National Association of Social Workers. (2004). www.socialworkers.org/practice/children/NASWChildWelfareRpt062004.pdf.

National Council of Juvenile and Family Court Judges (1999). Effective interventions in domestic violence and child maltreatment cases: Guidelines for policy and practice. Reno, NV: Author.

Ohio Department of Job and Family Services. (2006). Fiesel case review.

Osofsky, J. and Fenichel, E. (1994). *Caring for infants and toddlers in violent environments: Hurt, healing and hope.* Arlington, VA.

Post, Stephen. www.stephengpost.com

Purcell, Shaun. National Child Traumatic Stress Network, Boston University Medical Center Institute of Psychiatry, King's College London. University of Wisconsin-Madison.

Shonkoff, J. & Phillips, D. (Eds). (2000) *From neurons to neighborhoods: The science of early childhood development-an introduction.* Washington DC: National Academy Press.

US Census Bureau. (2006). wwwcnsus.gove/popest/national/asrh/NC-EST 2006-02.xls.